CW00685421

Cavern Club:
The Inside Story

These original labels were
produced in 1967, over 50 years
ago and were affixed to all Cavern
Club memorabilia mailed to the
four corners of the World.

CAVERN CLUB:
THE INSIDE STORY

Debbie Greenberg

JORVIK
P R E S S

ISBN-10: 0-9863770-4-X
ISBN-13: 978-0-9863770-4-4

Library of Congress
Catalog No: 2016950777

Cover photos: Earl Preston's Realms (courtesy
Nigel Greenberg), the Hollies and the Beatles
(courtesy Les Chadwick Peter Kaye Photography)
Cover design: Keith Carlson

First edition

Jorvik Press
5331 SW Macadam Ave., Ste. 258-424
Portland OR 97239 USA
JorvikPress.com

About the Author

Born in 1945 in Liverpool, Debbie Greenberg attended the Morrison School on Greenbank Road and, after passing her eleven-plus, New Heys High School for Girls.

Leaving school at seventeen, she started working with her father, Alf Geoghegan, who ran three butcher's shops. By age 20 she was managing the family business and also working part-time as a fashion model.

Her life changed forever when her father took over the lease of the Cavern Club in 1966 after the previous owner went bankrupt. Now she had to immerse herself in the running of the world's most famous club.

Debbie lives with her husband Nigel in Liverpool and partners with him in their 44-year-old business, Solo Security.

ACKNOWLEDGMENTS

With grateful thanks to Tim Mobbs, who rescued my manuscript from a crashed computer when all seemed lost; Ian Pennington for his expert IT help; Colin Hall for his editorial guidance in the early stages; and Frank Cottrell Boyce for pointing me in the direction of Jorvik Press.

For their professional expertise and valuable time I must also thank Daniella King and Alison Gorlov for invaluable advice and research; Margaret Roberts and Les Chadwick of Peter Kaye Photography for their generous help and kind permission to reproduce early photographs; Harry Lea of MPS Imaging for his expertise; Roger Hull at Liverpool Record Office; *Liverpool Echo* for permission to print article excerpts and photos; and Paul Wayne of Tracks Ltd.

Sam Leach, legendary Liverpool promoter, has always been there to share his memories and photographs with me, which I especially appreciate.

The current owners of the Cavern have helped me at every turn. Special thanks to Dave Jones, Bill Heckle and Jon Keats for their magnanimous assistance. And kudos to Peter Stansill and all at Jorvik Press for believing in me and allowing me the opportunity to tell my story.

Of course, acknowledgements would not be complete without a word of thanks to my husband Nigel, who has encouraged and supported me every step of the way and shared all his memories – he was, after all, at the Cavern even before I was. Many were the times during the writing of this book that he was prepared to live on anything that could be put on a piece of toast.

DG
Liverpool, 2016

*Dedicated with love
to my father,
Alfred Geoghegan*

CONTENTS

A Chance to Save the Beatles Shrine

I was twenty years old in March 1966 when my father said to me, "I've got the chance to buy the Cavern. What do you think?"

Oh my God, I couldn't believe my own ears. Was my Dad really considering buying the most amazing club on the planet? One which I had been fanatical about ever since my first visit in the late fifties when it was still a jazz club and where I had later witnessed the birth and the ultimate success of the Beatles?

Being what could only be described as a Cavern addict, who had hardly ever missed a lunchtime or evening session from the early sixties to its closure a few weeks before, my reply was swift and decisive.

"What do you mean, you don't know what to do? Take it! I've seen the Cavern at its peak and it could happen again."

My mother was amazed at his question.

"Fancy asking Deb! She practically lives in the place."

My grandmother, who lived with us, used to say, "I don't know why she doesn't take her bed down there."

Mother pointed out that it was a very serious matter and that all their life's savings would be going into the venture.

"Look, Dad, besides the fact that you would make me the happiest girl in the world, from a business point of view I really think it could be great again."

I was excited at the prospect but at the same time I realised how serious a step this was for him. My Dad and I shared an amazing degree of trust and were very close, especially as I was an only child. He knew I would only give him what I believed to be the right advice. Since I knew the Cavern well and realised its full potential he respected my judgement.

Just a few weeks before, on the 28th of February, the Cavern Club had been closed down after the owner, Ray McFall, could not pay his debts. It was a huge blow to the Cavern regulars, but now a life-line was being thrown out to save it – and my Dad was grasping at it.

I had read the article about the club's closure in the *Liverpool Echo* only days before on the 1st of March:

A HARD DAY'S FIGHT ON THE BARRICADES

One hundred and fifty teenagers locked themselves inside the world's most famous beat club and began a fantastic three-hour siege. They pulled down the roller shutter across the main entrance and piled chairs, tables and boxes against the entrance to form a barricade. They danced, sang and chanted inside the dimly lit cellar, as police and other officials tried to get in.

The battle was staged in a bid to prevent the shutdown of Liverpool's beat world mecca – the Cavern Club in Mathew Street, where the Beatles made their name.

It happened after club owner Ray McFall, 38, appeared at Liverpool County Court.

A receiving order was made against him for non-payment of £1,500.00 which he owed to a building firm for work done at the club. The official receiver stepped in to close down the cellar and signal the start of the siege of Mathew Street.

Youngsters, some of whom had been there since a marathon beat session started at 3 p.m. the previous day, Sunday 27th February, had defied the closing order and started to build the barricade. The time-table of the battle went like this.

10.03 a.m. The receiving order was issued.

10.30 a.m. Mr. McFall reports to the nearby Official Receiver's Office.

11.20 a.m. Word is received at the Cavern Club and barricades go up.

11.35 a.m. Mr. McFall arrives at the club with the Assistant Official Receiver Mr. Thomas Wilks and the Examiner Mr. R Morley. They can't get in.

11.50 a.m. Police arrive to clear more than 100 teenagers waiting outside the club.

1.05 p.m. Work starts on moving the tables and chairs blocking the steps into the Cavern – as the boys and girls sing the American freedom movement song, "We Shall Not Be Moved."

1.20 p.m. The teenagers give in. the Cavern is officially closed. But the teenagers, many of them having spent 20 hours below, had not finished their protest. They carried letters spelling out the word CAVERN in a march to the Town Hall.

Finally, the marchers, more than 300 strong, squatted outside the Cavern Club, still singing.

Again police moved in to clear the street, and at last the party was over – bar the talking. Talk about the famous stars that have appeared at the Cavern – the Beatles, Cilla Black, The Searchers, Billy J Kramer.

"They were wonderful years," said Mr. McFall, who admitted that he was £10,000.00 in the red. "The demonstration was fantastic but I had nothing to do with it. It was the kids' idea. Now it's all over I suppose I'll have to find a job."

Cavern disc jockey Bob Wooler said, "I can't believe it's all over. It's the end of an era."

A weeping Freda Kelly, 20, secretary of the Beatles' Fan Club in Liverpool, sobbed, "I'm broken-hearted."

And the last word from a policeman. "Talk about a hard day's night, but it's sad isn't it?"

In Spencer Leigh's 1984 book, *Let's Go Down the Cavern*, doorman Paddy Delaney remembers the club at its peak: "Virtually overnight the Cavern became very famous. Tourists were coming to Mathew Street and snapping this hole in the wall. It was only a doorway with no big sign and, as I had to stand on the door, people from all over the world were asking me questions.

"One American girl wanted to see the band-room. I pointed to where Ringo Starr always sat. She got down on her knees and kissed the spot and then she broke down crying. There were scenes like that every day of the week."

 TV programmes were filmed there – both British and French – and live recordings became EPs and albums. Local bands that had found national fame still came back to to play at the Cavern.

On 3rd August 1963 the Beatles had made their final appearance at the Cavern, the 292nd time they played there. Paddy Delaney remembers it well in *Let's Go Down the Cavern*: "The last time the Beatles appeared at the Cavern was for £20. The booking had been arranged months

A hard day's fight on the barricades

It's all over . . . and a broken hearted teenager is comforted by two friends.

ONE HUNDRED AND FIFTY teenagers locked themselves inside the world's most famous beat club yesterday . . . and began a fantastic, three-hour siege.

They threw chairs, tables and boxes against a door to form a barricade.

They locked a side gate leading to a fire escape.

They danced, sang and chanted inside the dimly-lit cellar, as police and other officials tried to get in.

The battle was staged in a bid to prevent the shut-down of Liverpool's beat-world mecca—The Cavern Club in Mathew-street, where the Beatles made their name.

Marathon

It happened after club-owner Ray McFall, 38, appeared at the city's county court.

A receiving order was made against him for non-payment of £1,500 which he owed a building firm for work at the club.

The Official Receiver stepped in to close down the cellar and signal the start of the siege of Mathew-street.

Youngsters—some of whom had been there since a marathon beat session started at

Story by
FRANK CORLESS

Pictures by
ALFRED MARKEY

3 p.m. on Sunday—defied the closing order, and started to build the barricade.

The timetable of the battle went like this:

10.03 a.m. The receiving order is issued.

10.30 a.m. Mr. McFall reports to the nearby Official Receiver's Office.

11.20 a.m. Word is received at the Cavern Club and the barricades go up.

11.35 a.m. Mr. McFall arrives at the club with the Assistant Official Receiver Mr. Thomas Wilks, and the Examiner Mr. R. Morley. They can't get in.

11.50 a.m. Police arrive to clear more than 100 teenagers waiting outside the club

1.05 p.m. Work starts on moving the tables and chairs blocking the steps into the Cavern—as the boys and girls sing the American "freedom" movement song "We Shall Not Be Moved."

1.20 p.m. The teenagers give in. The side

gate is opened. The Cavern is officially closed.

But the teenagers—many of them having spent 20 hours below—had not done.

They carried letters making out the word C A V E R N in a match to the town hall.

Finally the marchers—more than 300-strong — squatted outside the club still singing.

Again police moved in to clear the street. And at last the party was over . . . bar the talking.

'Fantastic'

Talk about the famous stars who have appeared at the "Cave"—the Beatles, Cilla Black, The Searchers, Billy J. Kramer.

"They were wonderful years," said Mr. McFall, who admitted he was £10,000 in the red.

"The demonstration was fantastic. But I had nothing to do with it. It was the kids' idea.

"Now it's all over, I suppose I'll have to find a job."

Cavern disc jockey Bob Wooler said: " I can't believe it's over. It's the end of an era."

A weeping Freda Kelly, 20, secretary of the Beatles' Fan Club in Liverpool, sobbed: " I'm brokenhearted."

And last word from a police-man: "Talk about a hard day's night. But it's sad, isn't it ? "

before but in the meantime they had risen to the top. They were making thousands of pounds, so their appearance at the Cavern was a big joke.

"The crowds outside were going mad. By the time John Lennon had got through a cordon of girls, his mohair jacket was minus one sleeve. I grabbed the sleeve to stop the girl getting away with a souvenir. I gave it back to John and the first thing he said when we got down to the band-room was, 'Has anybody got a needle and thread?' John immediately stitched his sleeve back on."

Until that fateful last night in February 1966 no one knew anything was wrong. It was just like any other Sunday night at the Cavern – until Ray McFall arrived and informed the staff that the bailiffs would be there the next morning. He said the club was to stay open all night – with free admission. Young men were furious, girls cried, and by the early hours patrons had blocked the stairs leading down to the club. No one could get in or out.

When the police arrived Paddy told the protesters to let them in. The kids were escorted out but they wanted doorman Paddy to be the last one to leave.

The two working directors of Cavern Sound Ltd., Nigel Greenberg and Peter Hepworth, whose recording studio occupied the basement of No. 8 Mathew Street, next door to the Cavern at No. 10, had no idea Ray McFall was about to declare bankruptcy when they locked up the previous Friday. The recording studio could only be accessed through the front door of No. 8, where the Cavern offices were situated.

Nigel recalls: "When we arrived for work that Monday we found that bailiffs, acting on behalf of the Official Receiver, were sealing up the front roller shutter to prevent anyone from removing any of Ray McFall's assets, which were to be sold to pay off his debts.

"I tried to explain to one of the bailiffs that Cavern Sound Ltd. was a completely separate legal entity to the Cavern Club and that none of the studio equipment belonged to Ray, but the bailiff would have none of it and prevented us from entering the building.

"Paddy Delaney, the legendary head doorman of the Cavern listened to my tale of woe over a pint of beer that lunchtime at the Grapes, the pub opposite the Cavern where all the groups used to drink. He was very sym-pathetic to our predicament and told us that he might have a solution.

CHAIRS BAR BAILIFFS *Defiant teenagers in a desperate last attempt to keep open the mecca of the Liverpool Sound barricade an entrance with tables and chairs and stage a sit-in.*

(Courtesy Liverpool Echo/Trinity Mirror)

"He remembered that during construction we had covered over an old metal door on the rear wall that led to a light-well, enclosed by the warehouses in Mathew Street and Harrington Street. This led to a rear passageway to the street, covered by an old metal barred gate and secured by an ancient rusted padlock." Paddy even offered to let Nigel and Peter use the van he drove to deliver copies of the local fortnightly music paper, *Mersey Beat*.

They manoeuvred the heavy studio equipment through the ancient light-well and out to the waiting van, which transported it to the garage at Nigel's mother's house in Allerton.

Nigel continues: "The following day we made our way back to Mathew Street where Ray and Bob where holding court in the Grapes, giving interviews to the national press. I think Ray was quietly thinking the Official Receiver would open up the club and remove anything of value, including our equipment. The contents of the Cavern offices were just a few desks and filing cabinets, but the studio equipment, expanded and upgraded over the years, was worth several thousand pounds.

The sit-down in Mathew Street after the Cavern was closed down
(*Courtesy* Liverpool Echo/*Trinity Mirror*)

"The bailiffs returned the next day to take inventory of everything that could be sold. They broke the seal on the shutter of No. 8 and the official party of six or seven, including ourselves, followed them into the Cavern offices. We listened as a bailiff called out: 'One office desk, five foot by three foot with drawers, one Disley four-drawer filing cabinet, one Underwood typewriter...' Then we moved on to the club proper, where they compiled a full inventory.

"Finally the bailiff said, 'Now for the recording studio.' I couldn't miss the grin on Paddy's face. We climbed the stone steps from the Cavern and went back into No. 8 and down to our basement studio. Dumbfounded, the bailiffs asked, 'Where is all the equipment you told us about, Mr. McFall?'"

Nigel adds: "I then announced, 'Mr. McFall does not own any equipment. All the equipment owned by Cavern Sound Ltd., which I bought with my own funds, has been removed. The Official Receiver has no legal claim to it.'

"'We'll see about that,' said the bailiff, but nothing further was ever heard from official channels."

Bob Wooler, always ready with a nickname, christened Nigel Mr. Moonlight for his moonlight flit with the recording gear.

Nigel Greenberg was born in 1942 in Southport, twenty miles up the coast from Liverpool. While at Toxteth Technical Institute he formed a skiffle group with friends, encouraged by the enormous popularity of Lonnie Donegan. At first he played the washboard but eventually convinced his mother to buy him a guitar.

His other passion was all things mechanical, electrical and electronic, so he applied his skills to build an amplifier to make the group's guitars sound like a proper pop group.

Nigel's connection with the Cavern went way back. "During my teenage years one of my close friends was Franklin Sytner," he recalls. "We shared an interest in skiffle, and some nights I would tag along with Frank to the Cavern club, which was then owned by his brother."

Frank's brother, Alan Sytner, had opened the premises in 1957 as a jazz club, but from the early 60s skiffle groups started playing. Alan eventually sold the Cavern to Ray McFall, who took over on 3rd October 1959 with Acker Bilk and his band top of the bill.

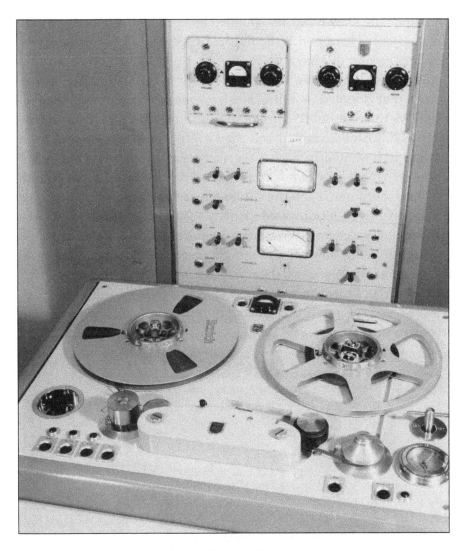

Cavern Sound's state-of-the-art gear

By 1961 the music scene in Liverpool was starting to take off. Hundreds of groups were playing in suburban dance halls and city centre clubs. Most bands were quartets – lead, rhythm and bass guitarists and a drummer. Each guitarist needed an amplifier and the group also needed a public address system with microphones and loudspeakers.

"We designed and built a few prototypes in our garage," says Nigel. "Then we approached a few local pop groups and two musicians tried our amplifiers, liked how they sounded and ordered two for £59 each. They were very happy with the finished product and we realised this could be the start of a lucrative business."

After installing a new sound system for Hope Hall, a city centre cinema that doubled as a live music venue, they were approached by Ray McFall and Bob Wooler to discuss a new venture. By 1963 the Beatles had made Liverpool and the Cavern world-famous, and now Ray and Bob wanted to open a recording studio in the vacant cellar next door, where local bands could record demo discs. Cavern Sound Ltd. was incorporated and the studio opened in late 1964.

Nigel explains: "It transpired that Ray's sound studio idea was a last-gasp attempt to generate additional revenue to prop up the club, which was rapidly going down the drain. He loved the limelight and even accompanied the Beatles on their first trip to the US at enormous cost.

"Ray always hinted in newspaper reports after his bankruptcy that he over-reached himself in financing the studio, when in fact he never invested a single penny."

Nigel Greenberg outside the Cavern Club.

Ray McFall's car outside the Cavern
(*Courtesy* Liverpool Echo/*Trinity Mirror*)

A Life of Hard Knocks

The new operator of the most famous club in the world was born Alfred Henry Geoghegan on 13th May 1909 in Shallcross Street, Everton. He was one of eight children who shared a happy yet disciplined upbringing. The family later moved to Kilshaw Street and then to Rocky Lane to a much larger house over a shop. Saturday evenings were spent playing the piano, singing and making music until the early hours. His mother, Emily, would make food for the whole family, plus cousins, who descended for the weekly party. His father, James, had been a captain in the army and was wounded at Passchendaele in the First World War.

Dad left school at fourteen and worked in a butcher's shop, Colburn's in West Derby Road. Reportedly, owner Jack Colburn took the bus every night for a few stops before alighting near his waiting Rolls Royce to be driven home by his chauffer. He clearly didn't want his staff or customers to know how well he was doing.

Dad started by delivering orders by bicycle and eventually worked his way up to become a qualified butcher, but a terrible accident on the bacon slicer deprived him of the little finger and ring finger on his right hand. One of the juniors had altered the slicer speed to the fastest setting and Dad hadn't used the guard. He was rushed to hospital but the doctors were unable to save his fingers.

In excruciating pain for months and out of work, he eventually received £1,000 compensation from his boss's insurance company and bought a motorbike with some of the money.

At twenty-six in 1935 he met my mum, Laura Wilson. She was working in the shoe department at Henderson's department store in Liverpool. A friend she worked with was meeting a boy after work who also rode a motorbike, so my dad tagged along. He was instantly smitten and kept turning up at the store after work to ask her out.

With both the time and the money, he took her to Ireland for a three-month stay in 1936 to research his family tree. They made their

Geoghegan family crest

way around the country, starting in Dublin where his father was born, visiting town halls, libraries, churches and remote villages, knocking on people's doors in the Castletown Geoghegan area.

Miraculously they managed to trace his ancestors back to the year 400. Apparently there were two brothers, both provincial monarchs – King Naill McGeoghegan of the Nine Hostages and Fergal Roe McGeoghegan. Recent research suggests King Naill was responsible for bringing St. Patrick to Ireland as a slave.

Somewhere along the way the original McGeoghegan was reduced to Geoghegan. When I visited the Heraldic Shop opposite Dublin Castle in 1982 to order the coat of arms, they asked me if I was aware that not only was it a very old crest but a royal crest, featuring the lion rampant.

There were virtually no jobs Dad could do after his accident, so with a little money behind him he opened a book and took bets on the horses.

In the old country

Alf with motorbike, 1936

At that time off-track betting was still illegal, enabling a thriving trade in back-street bookmaking. My Aunt Alice, mother's sister, was the bookie's runner. She would collect bets from punters, mostly friends and neighbours, and tuck the betting slips and money under the baby blanket in the pram – with the baby on the top – to deliver to Dad for processing.

Dad was actually a frustrated jockey, 5 ft. 5 in. tall and the spitting image of the famous jockey, Gordon Richards. When he visited race-courses people would regularly approach him for an autograph.

When war broke out in September 1939, conscription was out of the question. He was rejected several times because he wouldn't be able to hold a rifle. He became a dispatch rider and, as one of his favourite pastimes was riding his Rudge motorcycle, it suited him well.

ENSA, Entertainment National Service Association or Every Night Something Awful, as it was fondly nicknamed, played a big part in his life during the war. His stage name was Arty Regan. He owned a George Formby ukulele and he and two other boys, Ernie and Big John, formed the Ukulele Rhythm Boys. They would travel the country entertaining the troops and were often on BBC radio's *Workers' Playtime* and *Music*

While You Work. He was also an amazing lightning cartoonist, his act consisting of topical cartoons drawn to music. Mum would accompany him on piano for the ENSA stage shows.

Dad loved the theatre and in 1940 wrote and produced a play called *On the Dole*, performed at a hired hall in Tuebrook, Liverpool, for one night. All the actors were dressed in Army uniforms and the play sold out. The public loved it and wanted him to run it again but he couldn't afford it.

Mum and Dad courted for five years before getting married at St. Silas's Church in High Park Street in 1940. They rented a semi-detached house in Pinehurst Avenue in Blundellsands, a North Liverpool suburb.

A few months before Christmas, Dad opened a shop at the bottom of Brownlow Hill to sell his hand-carved wooden toys. It didn't last long and he returned to butchering, renting a shop in Bootle with his brother

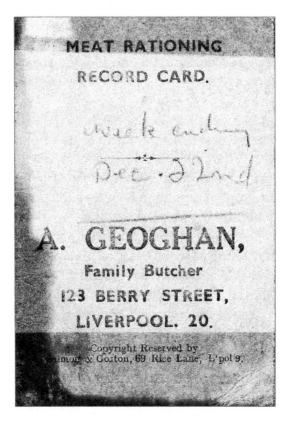

World War II meat rationing card

John. Bad luck struck again. The shop took a direct hit from the Luftwaffe during Christmas week and the huge meat fridge was buried under the rubble with just a corner protruding. All his customers' Christmas joints were inside. Undeterred, customers found a local man with a horse and cart and they all pulled together to free the fridge. Everybody got their Christmas dinner.

Liverpool played a huge part in the Battle of the Atlantic. In February 1941 Command Headquarters was relocated from Plymouth to Liverpool. Winston Churchill spent many days and nights there to be at the nerve centre of the operations. Consequently the city and its docks took a battering from German bombers, the most vicious campaign being the month-long May Blitz in 1941.

One of Dad's customers in Berry Street was an old lady who said she was Polish and who lived with her rather large, simple-looking son. They used to buy the cheapest cuts of meat and often beg a bone or two to make soup. One day the two of them were arrested and taken away, never to be seen again. The police had raided their dingy run-down house and discovered all sorts of radios and signalling equipment. It transpired that they were German spies.

With the war finally over, ever the inventor and entrepreneur, Dad invented a shoe polish that could turn brown shoes into black and black shoes brown with just one application. He would drive Mum mad by pinching her cooking pans to mix polish. He patented it as Bran-Nu.

Demand soon overtook supply, so he rented a factory in Jervis Street, Liverpool. He soon had dozens of girls working for him filling and pack-ing tins of polish. Then he opened a small factory in Broadstone in Dublin, Ireland, staying there during the week and flying home for weekends. His office was at the headquarters of his major client, the Tara Shoe Company, in Middle Abbey Street.

In 1948 he took a partner called Syd Smythe into the now thriving Bran-Nu business. Syd was to look after the Liverpool end of operations

Syd Smythe and girlfriend Sonja (right)

and to make sure market traders were well supplied. That was Dad's downfall. A few years later Syd asked Dad to buy him out and received £600 for his shares, a lot of money in 1950.

But Dad gradually became aware that cases of polish were stacking up, so he went to the markets to see what was wrong. The traders couldn't believe he was still in business. They told him Syd Smythe had said, "I've seen the writing on the wall, Bran-Nu is finished." Not only had this guy been absent from work entertaining his girlfriend at the Adelphi Hotel, but he had also screwed Dad out of £600 before he destroyed him.

Dad lost everything. He didn't realise that, as a limited liability company, he could have gone into voluntary liquidation; instead, he honoured all his debts. We lost our house in Salcombe Drive, most of its contents and the car, but my mother successfully fought with the bailiffs to keep her beloved piano, a wedding present from Dad.

With nowhere else to go, we had to pick up sticks soon after Christmas and go to live with my maternal grandmother in Princes Park. Up in the attic lay the remains of Dad's life at Bran-Nu in a small box on the floor covered in a thick layer of dust. Sticks of different coloured wax, empty polish tins, labels, a reference book for mixing polish and a small mixing bowl were all that was left of his multi-million-pound empire.

Dad picked himself up yet again and took a night job driving a black hackney cab. He soon saved enough to buy his own taxi and could again again afford a private school for me. He eventually sold his taxi, or so he thought, to a Mr. Murphy, who paid a deposit, took the log book from an over-trusting Alf and disappeared forever with the cab.

After a few years my nomadic mother decided we would all be better off living in the country. She had discovered what she called a "wonderful opportunity" in Wales some 90 miles from Liverpool. It turned out to be an absolute nightmare.

The wonderful opportunity was a butcher's shop attached to a house in a small village near Bangor in North Wales. I was eight when we arrived, the only English girl in the village school, ostracized and bullied for an entire year and a half. I also had to learn Welsh – at least I could understand the nasty things the other kids were saying.

My Dad worked like a slave. Not only did he run the shop but also drove the van to surrounding villages in all weathers, knocked on doors to take orders and butchered the meat on a small block in the back of the van.

After eighteen months of hell on earth, my mother's weight went down to six stone (38 kg). At the request of her mother, Mum's doctor travelled from Liverpool for a house call. He told Dad that if he didn't get her out of there within a month he'd be taking her out in a box.

Grandmother organised a furniture van to collect us. Once again we were inside the van on the settee, with the two dogs and Dad up front with the driver. Like a bad penny, we turned up again on my grand¬mother's doorstep in Princes Park.

My grandmother was an amazing woman. If anybody was giving birth she would be there to deliver the baby and if anybody died she would show up to lay them out. Small in stature, she had a temper that could flare and subside within minutes. With her wicked sense of humour and a playful streak, the two of us got on exceptionally well.

By contrast, my relationship with my mother was generally strained. She found it hard to show affection, probably because of her Victorian upbringing at her own grandmother's house. When I was young we had more of a teacher/pupil relationship rather than a mother/daughter bond, so I spent more time with my grandmother, with whom I had a wonderful relationship and loved dearly.

At the Morrison School in Greenbank Road, I couldn't believe how nice the girls were to me after the spitefulness and bullying I'd endured in Wales. It took me a long time to adjust and to trust. After passing the eleven-plus exam, I was awarded a place at New Heys High School for girls. I was twelve when I started in September 1957 and nearly seventeen when I left.

Dad worked for several years driving taxis to save enough to buy the first of our three butcher's shops, located in North Hill Street, South Liverpool. The shops were named Wilson's Butchers – Mum's maiden name – as most people couldn't pronounce Geoghegan.

People queued up to buy our famous sausages. Dad had been given the German recipe from an old butcher who was retiring. With sausage sales booming, he bought commercial equipment – a bowl chopper and a foot-operated filler that forced sausage meat through a nozzle and into the skins. It was fun making sausages – I could practically link them blindfolded. It never ceased to amaze me how my Dad could butcher as well as the next man, with only two fingers and a thumb on his right hand.

Debbie receiving her fashion modeling diploma

In July 1962 I left school and joined Dad full-time in the business. My mother was mortified that I'd chosen butchering over Art College. I had inherited my father's artistic leanings and was even interviewed by the Principal of Liverpool Art College. Although my drawings were good enough to secure me a place, I still wasn't interested.

Mum also arranged an interview at George Henry Lee's department store, as I'd expressed an interest in window dressing. I also fancied being a commercial artist until I found out what the requirements were. To me the best education was to be found in the school of life and I couldn't wait to leave school.

Actually, fashion was my passion. At nineteen I enrolled at the Patricia Platt modelling agency in Bold Street and in June 1967 passed my training course with an A-Plus diploma. I worked as a fashion model at shows and photo shoots while working in the butcher's.

Every Wednesday afternoon, half-day closing at the butcher's, I would take the bus into Liverpool and buy a yard of material from Blackler's department store to make a shift dress on my sewing machine to wear on Saturday night at the Cavern. This was how I came up with a new dress every week.

Girls were now wearing shift dresses just above the knee, with hemlines destined to rise as rapidly as Mary Quant's fame as a revolutionary designer. Liverpool girls were extremely fashion-conscious and eager to follow London trends.

It wasn't only the dress fashions that had a huge impact on young girls but also the iconic Mary Quant short-bobbed hairstyle. Girls flocked to salons to have their previously back-combed and bouffant tresses snipped away by scissor-happy stylists.

The idea of losing my long black waist-length locks gave me pause for thought. In late 1967 I did eventually succumb to the shorter style and walked into Peter Collinge's Hair Salon in Church Street. I went home with my hair in a bag. When I walked in with my new elfin hairstyle, Dad was mortified, Mum wasn't bothered one way or the other.

The next one in shock was my boyfriend, Alf. It wasn't long before I hated it too – I kept feeling for it on the pillow and felt very light-headed. Short black hair was not for me so I decided to go lighter and lighter until I reached blonde, and there I stayed.

The mini-skirt was born and was embraced by every shape and size of girl from John O' Groats to Land's End and, when complimented by a pair of shiny white pull-on stretchy plastic boots, the new look was complete.

Meanwhile, Dad had built up a thriving butcher's business, so his main concern was who would look after the shops and buy wholesale meat from the abattoir if he was going to run the Cavern Club. Having worked in the shop on Saturdays since I was twelve and full-time since leaving school, I volunteered to manage the lot while he and Mum ran the club.

The butcher's van

I regularly went with Dad to the abattoir and had worked my way
up to becoming a master butcher. Dad had taught me how to recognise
lean from fat when buying lambs and pigs, how to spot an old sow from
a young healthy pig, and how to tell bullock beef from cow beef.

He took me up on my offer. Suddenly at the age of twenty I was
thrown into managing three shops, ten staff plus a mobile butcher's
van, and doing all the buying at the abattoir twice a week – which involved rising at the unearthly hour of 4.30 a.m.

out a girl who leads a
uble life, yet none would
obably compare to the com-
ete contrast in the two lives
pretty 22-years-old Debbie
oghegan, of Greenbank
ad, Sefton Park.

Debbie has been a very
ccessful model for the past
elve months, appearing in
ows all over the country.
t, every morning, she dons
a familiar butcher's apron,
ns herself with knives and
oks, and sets to work in
r father's butchers shop,
Isons, in Camberley Drive,
lewood. Father is actually
. Alf Geoghegan, of the
vern Club.

Debbie at modelling photoshoot

Upgrading a 'Cellar Full of Noise'

It was Joe Davey who had first approached Dad about buying the Cavern. He owned Joe's Café, an all-night restaurant in Duke Street, where most of the groups and music fraternity congregated after gigs for something to eat in the early hours. It was open every day from 7.30 a.m. to 3 p.m. and every night from 10 p.m. until 4 a.m.

The Cavern was not only Liverpool's most popular beat music club. It was by then the most famous club in the world, the home of the Beatles who during the heady days of the early sixties had performed there almost three hundred times.

It was a magnet for teenagers hungry for their fix of the incomparable Mersey Beat sound and a mecca for the hundreds of groups that came to belt out their rock 'n' roll. Everybody wanted to go to the

Ray McFall and Bob Wooler

Cavern. It was addictive, a pleasurable, heady, feel-good drug – the more we got, the more we wanted.

However, by early 1966 the club was in trouble and rumours spread through the town that the Cavern was going to close. Ray McFall, who had given up a career as an accountant to run the Cavern, admitted, "I am in financial difficulties and owe a lot of money and my creditors are being patient but I am not selling out."

This, however, was not the case and McFall had to file for bankruptcy. He did not have the necessary funds to update drains, public access and ventilation, which Liverpool Corporation was now demanding, declaring the club was a potential death trap.

At the bankruptcy hearing the Judge told McFall, "You started out with the same opportunity as the Beatles." Then he asked why he had failed where they had succeeded.

When interviewed later, former Cavern office manager Bob McGrae and club DJ Billy Butler claimed the Cavern had been making money right up to the last minute but, owing to bad management and extravagance, the club's financial situation was completely haywire.

McFall had fallen under the spell of Beatlemania, insisting on accompanying the Beatles on their first trip to America, which was really only to satisfy his own vanity. Large sums of money had been transferred to prop up the magazine *Mersey Beat*, which McFall had purchased some years earlier from the founder, Bill Harry, a classmate of John Lennon's at Liverpool Art College.

Despite his training as an accountant, Ray was notoriously bad at keeping records both for *Mersey Beat* and the Cavern. The Official Receiver asked for offers for the lease and our offer of £5,500 was the highest bid received. Finally, on Monday April 18th 1966, my parents and Joe and Kath Davey took over the Cavern.

I will never forget that day and the mixed emotions among my family. I was ecstatic and couldn't contain my excitement. My mother, however, did not share my enthusiasm and faith in the project, but I knew Dad was quietly excited about what lay ahead.

"What have we done? We have poured all our life's savings into an old empty cellar," Mum moaned.

I could tell she was already regretting it. Dad was fifty-six years old when he embarked on this new venture, yet he had the determination and energy of an eighteen-year-old.

Once negotiations with the Official Receiver to take over the lease were concluded – and the cheque had cleared – Dad and Joe collected the keys. Now we were in business. This was the point at which dreams came face to face with reality.

With some trepidation, we opened up the door on the ground floor of No. 8 Mathew Street to find a reception desk area, several offices and a very dark and dusty space.

A corridor at the rear of the reception area led to four offices to the right. We were equipped with torches, as we didn't know where the light switches were. Dad found a switch in the corridor and tried turning it on but nothing happened. It was possible, we thought, that the electricity had been switched off at the mains but it was also possible that it had been cut off for non-payment. It was dark, cold, musty and damp.

We continued cautiously, one behind the other with our torches, and at the rear of the large empty space we discovered a wooden staircase which led down to the studio once occupied by Cavern Sound Ltd.

On ground level at the rear was a large metal door which, after several attempts to find the right key, we finally managed to open.

View from the Cavern stage

Behind it was an external light-well, no bigger than six by four feet, surrounded on three sides by sixty-foot-high walls.

To the left was a huge sheet of metal about ten feet high which, on closer inspection of the plans, revealed a concealed iron gate. This led down a 100-yard passageway to a T-junction with alleyways leading right to Harrington Street and left to Mathew Street, where metal gates secured the exits.

The smell of dead birds and bird droppings in this enclosed space was overpowering. At the risk of the smell following us, we left the door to the light-well ajar to throw some light into the rear of the building, as we continued our trek of discovery.

Descending the wooden staircase to the recording studio, we could immediately see that a lot of money had been spent to create a professional soundproof studio where many of the Liverpool groups had come to record demo discs.

Daylight hit us as we emerged from No. 8 on to Mathew Street. We then walked several yards down the street and Dad opened the roller shutter to No. 10, the main entrance to the club. Still by torchlight we descended the eighteen stone steps into the Cavern. For me it was re-entering a secret and wondrous place, a spine-tingling moment.

To actually own the Cavern was both magical and breath-taking. I had only been in the Cavern when it was full to bursting with people and pulsating with music. But even though it was eerie, empty and very smelly, this hallowed ground retained its mystique.

At the top of the stone steps I paused to remember how we would wait there, impatiently tapping our feet to the beat of the Mersey Sound, eager to reach the bottom and be part of the action. As we slowly descended, I was amazed to see that the small wooden table and chair that functioned as the pay desk were still in place, covered in dust.

The rows of wooden chairs in the central aisle facing the stage had been haphazardly replaced in untidy rows, probably after being used to barricade the main entrance the night the Cavern was closed down.

Either side of the central aisle were arched tunnels where, if you were lucky enough and early enough to grab a centre row seat, you could get a fabulous close-up view of the group on stage. You could practically touch them and also talk to them and make requests, with every performance like a private party.

The empty stage looked slightly eerie but in my mind's eye it was alive with a group rocking and bouncing around to the unmistakeable Mersey beat. Visions of the Beatles in their leather gear danced in my head.

Dad, not so overwhelmed by nostalgia, was eager to throw some light on our inspection. "Stay here while I see if I can locate the main switch board." He looked in cupboards behind the coffee bar but found nothing. He then found another cupboard under the stairwell.

"This looks promising." He opened it up.

"Yes, got it! Fingers crossed the electric hasn't been cut off."

We held our breath as he pulled the heavy metal lever down and cheered when the lights came on.

Pad and pen in hand, Dad was already working out what had to be done to make this place a success again. My mother followed us around in total disbelief, tut-tutting that he had been crazy enough to put their money into some dirty smelly old cellar. I had to smile inwardly at the look of utter disdain on her face as she struggled to come to terms with owning the Cavern.

Bob Wooler interviewing the Big 3
(photo courtesy Les Chadwick Peter Kaye Photography)

It did stink after being locked up for over a month with no disinfectant added to the toilets to mask the stench, but after a few swift inhalations you got used to it. I watched Mum's nose wrinkle in disgust at the smell. Nobody needed a closer look to actually check on the toilets – and anyway there was no going back now.

Joe and Kath Davey followed us around, taking everything in but not saying much. Kath looked just as bewildered as Mum. Joe, who couldn't write and who used to sign his cheques with a cross, relied totally on Dad to make notes and draw plans of the club.

It transpired that they had bought the lease of not just No. 10 Mathew Street, the original Cavern Club, but also No. 8 and No. 12. The site was enormous, stretching almost as far as The Grapes on the opposite side of the street, the pub where the Beatles and most of the Liverpool groups used to drink.

No. 12 Mathew Street was bricked up between the arches of the far left wall of the Cavern. We wouldn't have known that it existed but for the fact that we had a copy of the building plans. We decided to leave No. 12 sealed up for now. If we needed room to expand in the future, we had extra space available next to the old Cavern premises.

The small coffee bar at the front of the club was still in place, tired and dusty with plastic cups on the serving counter and litter strewn on

The Hideaways at the Cavern
(photo: Frankie Connor's personal collection)

the floor – remnants of the final marathon session on 28th February. Rodents had long since seen off any discarded food.

We made our way down the left tunnel to the band-room where, outside the door, was an upright piano. The bailiffs had either missed it or deemed it worthless. My sense of breathless anticipation returned. We followed Dad into the band room.

"Wow!" I was covered in goose bumps. This is where the Beatles and all those great groups had sat and joked with one another and changed into their stage clothes before climbing the two wooden steps through the arch on to the stage.

This was a first for me – I had never been in the band room, just sneaked an occasional peek from the tunnel. This tiny space, no bigger than eight by ten feet, oozed pure excitement. The walls were covered in signatures and quips from the Beatles, Gerry and the Pacemakers, the Mersey Beats, the Searchers, the Hideaways, the Fourmost, the Big Three, the Undertakers and many more. I was mesmerized by this scrawled record of rock history, which gave me hope that we could rekindle the spirit. Was this actually happening? Had Dad really bought the Cavern?

The turntable and microphone Bob Wooler used for announcements were still in place, under a dust blanket, to the right of the steps that led on to the stage. I couldn't resist climbing on stage. Looking out into the dimly lit tunnel where I had often been packed in with hundreds of other fans, I finally experienced the band's eye view of the Cavern.

The old cloakroom to the right of the stage, where Cilla Black used to take the coats, was still intact but Dad already had plans to relocate it upstairs in No. 8.

With all the light switches now working, we breathed a sigh of relief that we now had power in both buildings. Mum immediately contacted Merseyside and North Wales Electricity Board and asked them to send an inspector to read the meters to ensure we would only be liable for power consumed from that date.

Liverpool Corporation imposed strict conditions for building improvements. Most important was the provision of new toilets connected to the main drains and improved air extraction and ventilation so that it would no longer feel like a sauna when the club was full. Also crucial was a new emergency exit so patrons could be rapidly evacuated.

THE BEATLES FAN CLUB - ADVANCE INFORMATION

Details of the Beatles first performances in this country
after their return from Germany

Saturday	June 9th	Special 'Welcome home' performance at the Cavern.
Monday	June 11th	B. B. C. recording in Manchester "Here we go" (for transmission on Friday June 15th)
Tuesday	June 12th	Lunchtime and Evening at the Cavern
Wednesday	June 13th	Lunchtime and Evening at the Cavern
Friday	June 15th	Lunchtime and Evening at the Cavern
Saturday	June 16th	Evening at the Cavern
Tuesday	June 19th	Lunchtime and Evening at the Cavern
Wednesday	June 20th	Evening at the Cavern
Thursday	June 21st	Lunchtime at the Cavern
* Friday	June 22nd	Shrewsbury
* Saturday	June 23rd	Northwich
Sunday	June 24th	Casbah (West Derby)
* Tuesday	June 26th	Floral Hall Southport.
* Friday	June 29th	Tower, New Brighton
Friday	July 6th	Riverboat Shuffle on Mersey

* Subject to confirmation.

Alert to what was happening, the *Liverpool Echo* ran a very encouraging story with the news that the iconic Cavern Club had been rescued. Almost immediately most of the old staff members were knocking on the door hoping to get their jobs back.

First to arrive was Paddy Delaney, the legendary head doorman, closely followed by former DJ and compere Bob Wooler who had introduced the Beatles for their two hundred and ninety-two appearances. Billy Butler, also a former resident DJ, was not far behind. They were all welcomed and promised their old jobs back when we re-opened after renovation.

That afternoon I saw Bob Wooler return to the club and go into one of the offices. He started removing boxes containing LPs and what looked like files of documents and loaded them into a grey estate car parked outside. Nobody questioned him and it wasn't until much later that we realised some of the documents probably might have been related to the lease. We never saw them again.

Our investigative marathon was almost over. We had examined the layout, got our bearings and checked through the offices, with Dad scribbling away, redesigning and restructuring the building in his head. This was our first step on a long and exciting journey to resurrect the Cavern. It was now up to us to transform the dream into reality.

Smells, Sweat and Memories

There were no main drains in the Cavern, just a cesspit into which the toilets flowed, topped up with strong disinfectant by the cleaners each morning to disguise the smell. In the heady days of the early 60s the whiff of disinfected drains didn't seem to bother anybody.

Rivers of condensation ran down the walls and the odour of cigarette smoke permanently hung in the air. The strong smell of perspiration from hundreds of overheated people just added to the ambience. The smell of rotting fruit also drifted in from the Fruit Exchange across the street.

Mix into this the occasional lingering scent of new leather, worn by those who could afford it, and the tantalizing smell of hot dogs and soup from the café, and you had the odorous cocktail that helped to make the Cavern what it was: a wondrous place where teenagers could escape.

For the crowds of excited teenagers that thronged the tiny space the pulsating beat was all that mattered. The throbbing music was so loud you couldn't hear yourself think, let alone speak.

Typical night at the Cavern
(photo courtesy Les Chadwick Peter Kaye Photography)

Everybody would perspire but most of the regulars would not take off their coats. It just wasn't the cool thing to do. The music penetrated every cell in your body, and we couldn't get enough of it. It made the Cavern the most magical place on the planet.

As soon as you entered Mathew Street you could hear and feel the throb of the music, like a giant heart beating inside the Cavern. Long before you descended the narrow staircase into the club your pulse was racing. Like everyone else, I couldn't wait to get in on the action.

Young, carefree and reckless, we never stopped to think as we descended into the bowels of the earth that in the event of a fire or other emergency, the club would have been a death trap for hundreds of young people pushing up that very narrow staircase to the street. There was never the luxury of a fire escape at the Cavern. Thinking about this fifty years later is very sobering.

In the early 1960s girls' make-up consisted of heavy black eye liner, false eyelashes, no lipstick (just pan-stick on their lips) and very pale faces. Nobody wore blusher or lipstick or any shade of colour on their cheeks. Most girls had beehive hairstyles back-combed and lacquered into the highest of domes, sometimes worn with a full fringe but usually with a centre-parted draped fringe. Beehive hairstyles were all the rage and girls would compete to build the highest stack of hair.

Black polo necked sweaters and black tights with knee-length pencil skirts or skinny black trousers and duffle coats was the girls' usual attire. Winkle-picker shoes were a must. I had two pairs, one metallic grey and the other metallic bronze. Most of the boys also wore duffle coats, black polo-necked sweaters and dark trousers. The obligatory Ban the Bomb badge was more of a fashion statement than a serious political message for most of us.

In 1962, I was lucky enough to own a three-quarter-length black leather coat; it was as soft as butter and I wanted to wear it forever. My friend Sue had a similar length coat in brown suede.

Some people did take off their coats when it got too hot but we never did. There was a cloakroom to the right of the stage where Cilla Black often worked during the second lunch-time session. She got five bob (25p) an hour for hanging coats. It amused her later to read in American magazines that she had been the "hatcheck girl" at the

JULY 18—AUGUST 1, 1963   MERSEY BEAT   PAGE 11

THE NORTH'S FIRST AND FOREMOST BEAT CENTRE

CAVERN CLUB

10 MATHEW ST. LIVERPOOL - CEN. 1591

FRIDAY, 19th JULY

FARON'S FLAMINGOS
(ORIOLE RECORDING ARTISTES)
DERRY AND THE PRESSMEN

THE MERSEY BEATS
(FONTANA RECORDING ARTISTES)

LEE SHONDELL AND THE BOYS

SATURDAY, 20th JULY

STEVE ALDO AND THE CHALLENGERS
THE FOUR JUST MEN
THE PANTHERS

SUNDAY, 21st JULY

Parlophone hit Recorders of "JUST LIKE ME"—

THE HOLLIES

THE SENSATIONAL VOCAL GROUP—PYE RECORDING ARTISTES

THE CHANTS

THE DEL RENAS

TUESDAY, 23rd JULY

THE HOLLIES
VINCE RENO AND THE SABRES

WEDNESDAY, 24th JULY

THE DENNISONS
(DECCA RECORDING ARTISTES—CURRENT RELEASE "BE MY GIRL")

THE CONNOISSEURS

FRIDAY, 26th JULY

RORY (DR. FEELGOOD) STORM
& THE HURRICANES

THE MERSEY BEATS

THE PANTHERS

SATURDAY, 27th JULY

MARK PETERS
AND THE
SILHOUETTES
Oriole recording artistes
CURRENT RELEASE—"FRAGILE"

THE FLINTSTONES

THE DETONATORS

Your host and compere

BOB WOOLER

SUNDAY, 28th JULY

THE DENNISONS
(DECCA RECORDING ARTISTES—CURRENT RELEASE—"BE MY GIRL")

THE MERSEY BEATS . RED RIVER JAZZ MEN

TUESDAY, 30th JULY

FABULOUS "MERSEY BEAT"
PACKAGE SHOW—

PYE RECORDING ARTISTS
JOHNNY SANDON
AND THE
REMO FOUR
(CURRENT RELEASE " LIES ")

PLUS

THE CHANTS

CAVERN STOMP

Yes, it's that fabulous "Cavern Stomp" the great new dance
born in Britain's leading beat centre, featured on TV. and on
record—Buy your copy of "The Cavern Stomp" (Decca) by
"The Big Three" and come down to the club and have fun.

Cavern, as people in Liverpool would only wear hats when they went to church – and certainly not in the Cavern.

The band room to the left of the stage was where Bob Wooler made announcements over the PA system. Beside him was the single turn-table where he played the latest records in the breaks while groups were setting up equipment.

My mother was so disturbed that I was spending every minute I could down at the Cavern that one night she persuaded Dad to go with her to lie in wait at the top of Mathew Street to catch me coming out of the club. She wanted to see what or who was the big attraction in this cellar that had such a hold on me.

They arrived home to find my grandmother waiting. "There's no sign of Deb, we couldn't see her anywhere." Mum was anxious.

"That's because she's in bed, she came home over half an hour ago," grandmother informed her with much satisfaction. "You know, Laura, you should learn to trust Deb, you should know she wouldn't go anywhere that was dangerous."

They never questioned me again about the Cavern. They just accepted the fact that it was the most amazing place in the world to me and not the den of iniquity my Mum had imagined.

One vivid memory is of an unusual regular Cave dweller (as Bob Wooler christened us) called Basil, or Baz as everybody called him. He worked for the city as a refuse collector (bin man) and was proud of it. We all liked him, though he was a little odd but completely harmless.

Some of the girls would cringe if he came to ask for a dance, because he would attract unwelcome attention with his dancing, arms and legs waving around in all directions with no sense of rhythm. We found the best way was to say hello and dance with him so he'd move on – if you ignored him he kept coming back. There was no escape from Baz.

My love affair with the club actually began when I first went to an evening session in December 1960, over five years before my Dad bought it. I was fifteen and immediately hooked. No alcohol was served, just Coca Cola and soup. Jazz bands were still playing at the Cavern, including the Merseysippi Jazz Band, Kenny Ball and Acker Bilk (who always had a pint of beer within easy reach on stage).

In 1956 a twenty-one-year-old Liverpool man, Alan Sytner, who had been running a weekly jazz club at several other Liverpool locations,

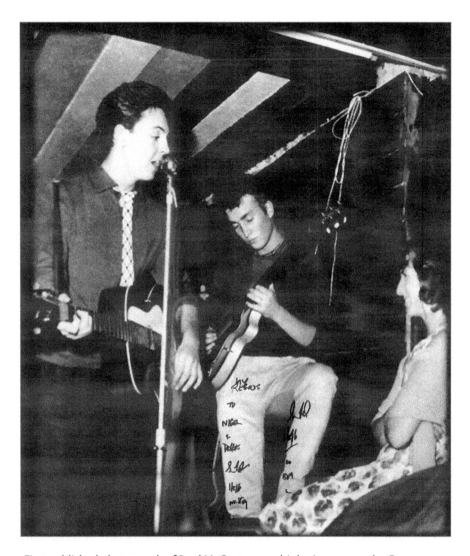

First published photograph of Paul McCartney and John Lennon as the Quarrymen,
with Cynthia Lennon, Aug 29, 1959 (photo Dick Matthews, © Sam Leach)

decided he would like to open his own club. He had been impressed by
a club he had visited on the Left Bank in Paris called Le Caveau, which
was housed in an underground cellar with brick arches.

On his return to Liverpool he sought out similar premises in the city
centre and found what he was looking for in Mathew Street, a narrow
street with warehouses on one side and the Fruit Exchange on the other.

It had previously been used for storage and even as an air raid shelter in World War II.

The cellar was painted, lighting was installed and a stage was built at the far end of the middle one of three tunnels. On Wednesday January 16th 1957 the Cavern Club opened for its first gig, with 600 people crammed inside – and 1,500 left outside. The headline act, the Merseysippi Jazzmen, are still performing today.

Alan Sytner ran the Cavern strictly as a jazz club but starting in 1957 he allowed skiffle groups to play, getting very annoyed if any of them tried to play rock 'n' roll. The Quarrymen skiffle group, precursor to the Beatles, first played the Cavern on a date no-one can pinpoint in mid-1957 and again on 7th August 1957, only weeks after John met Paul at the St. Peter's Church Garden Fete in Woolton Village.

John upset Sytner by playing rock 'n' roll numbers. Paul didn't appear with them, though he'd just been recruited. He was away at Scout Camp with his brother Mike in Hathersage, Derbyshire. While at camp, Mike broke his arm when he fell out of an oak tree he was climbing.

Interest in skiffle declined rapidly by the end of 1957 but remained popular as live entertainment for a while longer in Liverpool. On 31st July 1957 the Eddie Clayton group qualified for the final of the Cavern's summer skiffle competition. The Bluegenes also qualified. No one remembers who won. That was a big night as it featured the Miss Cavern beauty contest. Ringo and his mates in the Eddie Clayton group were too drunk to remember. Despite being underage they'd "grab a pass-out, go to the pub and then go back in – and pass out."

Their regular drinking haunts were the Lisbon on Victoria Street and the Beaconsfield on North John Street, according to Ray Trafford, Ringo's best mate and tea-chest bass player in the group. They drank black velvets, a cocktail of draught Guinness and sparkling wine, or rum and blackcurrant if they were flush. Ringo was the first Beatle to play the Cavern – but only by one week. As the Quarrymen, they last played the Cavern in Spring 1958.

In 1959 Alan moved to London and left his father, Dr. Joe Sytner, to run the club until a buyer could be found. Ray McFall was a clerk with the Sytner family's accountants and occasionally sat in at the Cavern cash desk. His offer of £2,750 to buy the club was accepted, and he officially took over the Cavern on 31st October 1959.

Queueing outside Cavern, 1962
(*photo courtesy* Liverpool Echo/*Trinity Mirror*)

Jazz bands appeared occasionally up to 1960, but it wasn't long before the beat groups infiltrated. American musical influence was fast taking hold on this side of the pond and the Cavern rapidly became a rock 'n' roll club. With no major pop radio stations in Britain, records brought home from America by Scousers working on ships were always in demand.

In case you don't know, a Scouser is a nickname for someone born and raised in Liverpool. We're named after a local dish, scouse, a stew made from vegetables and cheap cuts of meat, mainly lamb, a favourite of working-class families. There's also a dish called blind scouse, which has no meat.

I couldn't get enough of the Cavern, I would go there for every lunchtime session from Tuesday to Friday. There were two sessions, from 12 to 1 p.m. and 1.15 to 2.15 p.m. The later one was always the best – and then I would go back again at night for more.

We were greedy for our fix of non-stop beat music. The club didn't look like much from the outside. After dodging the fruit lorries delivering fruit to the Fruit Exchange opposite and the lunchtime shoppers, we queued to get in through a small door in the wall of a towering brick warehouse at 10 Mathew Street.

Once inside we descended a steep flight of well-worn stone steps to a small landing, where a few more steps led to a man seated at a small wooden table taking the entrance fees. I paid an extra shilling to become a member of the Cavern Club entitling me to an admission discount at each visit – which in my case was most days. The heat and noise would

Beatles on stage
(photo courtesy Les Chadwick Peter Kaye Photography)

send your senses reeling as you stepped through those cellar arches. It was enthralling and unbearably hot.

The Cavern's identity began to change at the start of the new decade. Rock 'n' roll slowly replaced jazz and the Cavern became the heart that gave Mersey its beat.

We watched the Beatles debut at the Cavern at the lunchtime session on 9th February 1961. We were blown away. The Beatles were different,

(Beatles photo courtesy Les Chadwick Peter Kaye Photography)

their music was incredible, their appearance raunchy, their energy infectious. They just oozed excitement.

Six weeks later on the 23rd of March, after a lunchtime session at the Cavern, they jumped on a train at Liverpool's Lime Street station on their way to Hamburg for the second time, having previously played there in 1960. This time they sped off out of our lives for four months. We missed them but still went down to the Cavern to watch other groups, like Gerry and the Pacemakers, the Swinging Blue Genes, the Remo Four, the Big Three, Kingsize Taylor and the Dominoes and many more. They were all fabulous groups but they weren't the Beatles.

News soon spread around Liverpool that the Beatles were back from Hamburg and were to be guests of the Swinging Blue Genes at the Cavern on Friday 14th July 1961 for their welcome home appearance.

Everybody wanted to see them. They were already by far the best group in Liverpool. Everything about them was exciting and intoxicating. They seemed to be infused with even more vigour and passion than before. The transformation was unbelievable, with their gyrating hips, humorous banter on stage and sexy outfits – clad in tight black leather with black Cuban heeled boots.

Their repertoire was now wide-ranging, making them stand out from other bands. Their sound was unique and addictive, their energy palpable. Liverpool had never seen or heard anything quite like them.

Sue and I made sure we were at the Cavern for every one of their performances after that. They appeared every Wednesday night and every Monday, Wednesday and Friday lunchtime.

The Hamburg connection proved the ultimate testing ground for many Liverpool groups. On some nights, groups would be expected to play at the Top Ten Club or Kaiserkeller or later on the Star Club for up to seven hours with only a ten-minute break every hour.

Those sessions transformed Liverpool groups into totally professional outfits. None more so than the Beatles. It turned them from talented amateurs into the band of bands, as Klaus Voormann described them. The Cavern was soon packed every time they played.

Bob Wooler booked them and they received £5 for their debut (£1 each). At that time Stuart Sutcliffe was playing bass guitar, although not very well, and he would often play with his back to the audience so no one could see how he was playing.

Tony Sheridan playing with the Beatles
(© Getty Images)

They had played a few numbers with Tony Sheridan in Hamburg, including "Ain't She Sweet," but the one that sticks in my memory is "My Bonnie." When the Beatles played these songs at the Cavern they were absolutely brilliant. I think Tony had a big influence on how the Beatles dressed and moved. John Lennon copied Tony's posture, holding the guitar high up on his chest.

Tony was very talented but by all accounts a force to be reckoned with. His mood could change in an instant. It must have been difficult to work with somebody so unpredictable. They had first met when both were playing for a season at the Top Ten Club in Hamburg. German band leader Bert Kampfert had spotted them and arranged for them to cut a disc of My Bonnie together, which was released in Germany.

News of this record filtered back to Liverpool and one fateful day, Saturday 28th October 1961, a Liverpool teenager called Raymond Jones went into NEMS record store to asking about the disc. Situated on Whitechapel, NEMS was just a stone's throw from Mathew Street and the Cavern. The young store manager was Brian Epstein, who prided himself on being able to source any record that had been officially released. After hearing the track with its throbbing beat he was intrigued.

Beatles' first manager Sam Leach with Dick Matthews,
John Lennon and George Harrison at the Palais Ballroom, Aldershot
(photo: Paul McCartney, © Sam Leach)

He asked his assistant, Alistair Taylor, to arrange a visit to the nearby Cavern to see the Beatles at one of the lunchtime sessions. He got there on 9th November 1961 with Alistair and saw the Beatles play for the first time.

He was entranced by their performance – and by the Cavern, the place he later called a "cellar full of noise."

However, Brian Epstein was not the first candidate for the position of Beatles manager. A Liverpool-based promotor called Sam Leach, who regularly organised dances and live shows in local venues, frequently hired the Beatles. As he was giving them regular work and they were all very good friends, he suggested he should become their manager.

The group agreed and on the strength of a hand shake with John Lennon, the group's leader, he thought he'd secured the position as their first manager.

On the 9th December 1961 Sam booked the Palais Ballroom in Aldershot, about forty miles outside London. He paid for a full-page ad in *The Aldershot News* and expected a good turnout for the gig. However, he had paid by cheque and the newspaper would not insert the ad until the cheque had cleared.

The cheque didn't clear in time and on that night only eighteen people turned up to see the Beatles.

After the hiccup at Aldershot everything was going very well for a few weeks until Brian Epstein stepped into the frame. The Beatles, ever eager to climb the ladder of success, were tempted by Brian's obvious wealth and promises of fame and fortune. With a heavy heart John Lennon had to break the news to Sam that they had signed with "Eppy."

Eppy was attracted to the group not just for their music; he was besotted by their personalities and he was especially attracted to John. As a closet homosexual he was all too aware that his sexual preference was still a criminal offence. But he had the skills, contacts and commitment to help them succeed.

After becoming their manager he vowed to get them a recording contract through his connections in the music scene. After many initial rejections he finally succeeded.

Overnight the Beatles had a following of devoted fans and I was one of them. The amazing thing about the Cavern was that the Beatles and all the groups were so accessible. We were literally inches away as they played.

The Beatles rehearsing on the Cavern stage
(photos courtesy Les Chadwick Peter Kaye Photography)

Filming A Hard Day's Night

The girls went crazy when Pete Best was sacked and replaced by Ringo. Pete was sultry, fiercely good-looking and oozed sex appeal. They would heckle the Beatles when they were on stage, shouting, "Pete forever, Ringo never." We were all outraged and couldn't understand why Ringo was the new drummer. The sound didn't seem any different to us.

Rumours about Pete's dismissal circulated around Liverpool. Some said he was too good-looking and Paul was jealous because he was getting the most attention from the girls. Others said Brian Epstein had decided his drumming wasn't good enough. I don't suppose any of us will ever get to the bottom of it; even Pete Best didn't know why he was dropped.

The Beatles inspired many groups to embrace rock 'n' roll – and they all wanted to play the Cavern. The resident DJ, Bob Wooler, would always introduce the show with, "Hi there, all you cave-dwellers. We've got the Hi-Fi high and the lights down low." At the end of the night he always played "I'll Be There" by Bobby Darin and we all knew it was time to leave. It was never the signal to get romantic as it was in other clubs. It was just time to go and catch the last bus home.

Bob later said, "The Cavern was the greatest finishing school pop music had ever known." How right he was. Garston-born Bob compered

The Hollies
(photo courtesy Les Chadwick Peter Kaye Photography)

around Liverpool for four years before giving up his day job as a British Rail clerk to go full-time as a DJ in 1960.

His first gig was at Litherland Town Hall on Dec 27th 1960, the first major show the Beatles played on their return from their first Hamburg trip. They delivered an incendiary performance, the like of which Liverpool had never seen before.

He would go on to compere lunchtime and evening sessions at the Cavern from 1961 until it was closed in early 1966. In a 1973 interview with Don Smith of the *Liverpool Daily Post*, Bob remembered, "It was dirty. It was incredibly noisy. It stank to high heaven. But it put Liverpool on the map so far as teenagers throughout the world were concerned. It was not just a place but an experience, a revolution. I should know, I saw it through the halcyon years, right through to the bankrupt years. Fed up with my job as a railway clerk, I took a chance and jumped down into the Cave, as I still call it, as a part-time, lunchtime disc jockey and compere. I found myself in a different world. I stayed in it for seven years. The happiest years of my life."

"A lot of rubbish has been written about the place, mostly by people who had either never been in it, or spent a few minutes there before dashing out, deafened. People said it made a fortune, that it led youngsters astray, that it was a vice midden. It was far from that. And it never, as has been suggested, exploited the penniless pop groups that queued to play there.

"It's true the Beatles played their hearts out for a quid each a night, but there was nowhere else for them to play anyway and they and the groups that followed were glad of the chance. I compered exactly 292 Beatle shows down in that sweaty hole. They loved every minute of it, so did the kids, and remember it was the kids who made the Cavern, not the Beatles, or the long line of groups that followed on.

"Ray McFall, who brought the club to its peak in 1964, was the man who could have made a fortune but went bust instead because he refused to charge youngsters more than a shilling a time if they were members and he refused to charge more than a shilling a year for membership. As a result the rent man was always at the door and we were number one in the writ parade. We were always in trouble.

"The businessmen around Mathew Street who employed the little girl clerks and their boyfriends went frantic because the youngsters would disappear for a couple of hours each day to listen to the lunch-time sessions. But what it did was to give these youngsters, whether schoolkids, underpaid clerks or messenger boys, an outlet and an insight into a less unhappy world.

"It is difficult to get the scene across now. The years have changed it, but I shall never forget the happy faces of those youngsters as they rocked and stomped their lunchtimes away. Remember there was no booze, they drank pop or Coke. Now you have a club on almost every street corner in the city centre with a disco and booze. They were fascinating days. Something new and almost unbelievable happened which had brought a lot of fun into a lot of lives.

"An industry was born. Work it out for yourself. This escape from the humdrum gave work to almost penniless but musically minded pop groups, the Beatles among them. Around 1964 we had more groups on Merseyside than we had dock strikes. The Beatles, the Searchers, Gerry and the Pacemakers, Cilla Black, The Bluegenes (and that was how they spelled their name originally) hit the headlines and the record sales almost everywhere and brought a lot of cash into this country.

"So now the old Cave is finished. I think it really finished in 1966 when Ray McFall, the man who people said was making a mint out of the place and the kids, went bust. It has never been the same since. I recall the nights when, with all night sessions, 12 local groups would carry on for 12 hours with up to 900 youngsters sticking it out and in what amounted to a steam bath by the end of the session. I don't think there was any chance of health hazards – no germs could have withstood the noise.

"It was murder. The place was a maze of tunnels and as the young-sters in one tunnel breathed in, the ones in another tunnel had the chance to breathe out.

"It was obvious it could not last. Groups became jealous of each other when one of them released a record. The beat which may have sounded discordant to the older generation was nothing to the discord which arose between the lads and the growing number of club owners. I am not just talking about the Beatles, although I think they have sadly moved from crepe soles to Crepe Suzette. They were great and I will never forget those early days when they were happy lads, stony broke and I not much better off, knew that they would make the top, but the Beatles didn't make the Cavern, the kids did.

"Strange, I thought, that no-one invited me to the last farewell..."

From 1961, I was down at the Cavern at every opportunity. When working in the butcher's shop I couldn't wait for one o' clock so I could hang up my coat and apron and run down North Hill Street to catch the bus into town for the lunchtime session. I would meet up with my friend Sue, who worked at a hairdresser's, and we would leg it to the Cavern and join the queue.

There were two sessions, the first at noon and the second at 1.15. I went to the later ones because they were always the best. At 1 p.m. everyone had to leave so the new crowd could file in. We often saw the Beatles, Gerry and the Pacemakers and Billy J Kramer at lunchtime and then returned at night to see one or more of them again.

We even cut short a week's holiday at the Butlin's Holiday Camp in Pwllheli in North Wales to get back to the Cavern, so strong was its pull. Before we left Butlin's we were asked by other teenagers to teach them the Cavern Stomp, a dance peculiar to the club.

Cilla Black with the Remo Four, Billy J Kramer with the Dakotas, and the Foremost
(photo courtesy Les Chadwick Peter Kaye Photography)

I suppose it was like a reverse jive. You held your partner by the hands, with shoulders hunched low and arms pointing straight down. While swaying and stepping from side to side to the beat, arms were gradually lifted in an upward swaying motion and then both parties would twirl together with arms in the air, still holding on to each other, and then repeat the downward sway.

One of the best songs to do the Cavern Stomp to was "Do You Love Me" by Faron's Flamingos and "Some Other Guy" and, of course, "The Cavern Stomp" by the Big Three. The songs and the dance were made for each other.

All the boys were copying the Beatles, growing their hair long and mimicking their wild head shake. As the Sixties progressed The Beatles and the Mersey Sound became a national phenomenon.

Girls all wore their hair long with a fringe like Cathy McGowan, who presented the popular TV music programme *Ready, Steady Go*. The Beatnik look of the early sixties had long been replaced by a more demure style of knee-length shift dresses for the girls and open-necked shirts with trousers and leather jackets for the boys.

Mersey Beat's Popularity Poll published in January 1962 by the *Liverpool Echo* had this Top Twenty based on reader's votes.

1 The Beatles
2 Gerry and the Pacemakers
3 The Remo Four
4 Rory Storm & the Hurricanes
5 Johnny Sandon & the Searchers
6 Kingsize Taylor & the Dominoes
7 The Big Three
8 The Strangers
9 Faron's Flamingos
10 The Four Jays (later the Fourmost)
11 Ian and the Zodiacs
12 The Undertakers
13 Earl Preston & the TT's
14 Mark Peters and the Cyclones
16 Derry and the Seniors
17 Steve and the Syndicate
18 Dave Fenton and the Silhouettes
19 Billy Kramer and the Coasters
20 Dale Roberts and the Jay Walkers.

Note that Billy Kramer had yet to find his middle 'J' and was still only 19th in the poll. He later swapped Liverpool's Coasters for Manchester's Dakotas, formerly fronted by Pete McLain.

One of my most treasured memories dates back to Friday 12th October 1962. We saw The Beatles at the Cavern lunchtime session and in the evening took the ferry across the Mersey to see them again at The Tower Ballroom in New Brighton. There were 12 groups appearing that night from 7 p.m. till 1 a.m., headlined by Little Richard, and it cost the princely sum of 10/6 (55p).

The Beatles with Little Richard at the Tower Ballroom, New Brighton
(photo courtesy Les Chadwick Peter Kaye Photography)

The Tower Ballroom was the polar opposite of the Cavern, a huge round amphitheatre with stairs leading up to a wide balcony walkway, where you had a bird's eye view. The stage was vast and at least five feet above the dance floor but lacked the personal touch of the Cavern. There were no seats and people just danced when the groups played.

The Empire Theatre in Liverpool also staged some fabulous shows in the early sixties. The Beatles' career was really taking off and they appeared on Sunday 28th October 1963. What a line up it was: Little Richard, the Beatles, Craig Douglas, Kenny Lynch, Jet Harris and the Jet Blades, the Breakaways and Sounds Incorporated.

My Dad's butcher's shop was on North Hill Street, diagonally opposite Admiral Grove, where the future Ringo Starr lived, though we still
knew him as Richie Starkey. He was born in Madryn Street but spent
most of his formative years at No. 10 Admiral Grove.

His mother, Elsie, was a friendly lady who would drop by our shop
every Saturday morning on her way to work, place a ten shilling note on
the counter and say, "The usual Deb. Our Richie will collect it this afternoon." Her order was always the same, half a leg of lamb and a quarter
pound of boiled ham.

Richie would arrive late afternoon and stand by the shop door, too
shy to come in. "Have you come for your Mum's meat, Richie?" I would
ask. He would nod, take the parcel and change and head home across
the street.

Most Saturday evenings after close of business Dad would treat our
butcher boys to a round of drinks at the Lothian Pub near Admiral
Grove. Before Richie joined The Beatles, he would sometimes sit in the
pub's small snug and my Dad occasionally offered him a drink. "Thanks,
I'll have a half," he would reply.

A few years later, after the Beatles had hit the big time, they all drove
up North Hill Street in a convertible, slowing down by Admiral Grove.
I was on the pavement, dressed in my butcher's coat and apron, as
crowds gathered to see the Fab Four. Even though their convertible was
travelling slowly behind a mobile film crew, the appearance was over in
a flash.

In 1958 we moved to Macket's Lane in Woolton, a lovely rural setting
that then faced open farmland. We used to watch farmers harvesting
in the evenings with tractor headlights full on. We had a clear view of
Runcorn Bridge from our front room. Everything changed when Ford
Motors opened a car plant in Halewood and Liverpool Corporation
built houses on the farmland. These estates housed hundreds of Ford
employees, many of whom moved from the inner city.

A family that moved into 174 Macket's Lane in August 1962 was
Louise and Harold Harrison and their sons, Peter and George, and
daughter Louise.

Mum took the bus home from the shop in North Hill Street. Long
before the Beatles were famous, Mum would often walk home from the
bus terminus with Mrs Harrison and they became firm friends.

When the Beatles were in the charts and making their last appearance at the Cavern, they all visited George's house. Mum called in to see
Louise and asked her if she could get the boys to sign some photographs
for her. Mum said there was a full size blown-up photograph of George
at the top of the stairs, which you couldn't miss when she opened her
front door.

Louise was a lovely lady and extremely proud of George. She invited
Mum into the living room where her husband sat at a small dining table
reading his newspaper. A milk bottle and a jar of jam sat comfortably
beside his cup of tea. Louise promised to ask the boys to sign photos
for her when they called in after their gig at the Cavern. They signed
four photographs for Mum. Later I generously and foolishly sent them
to friends of mine around the globe. Isn't hindsight a wonderful thing?

As the Beatles' popularity grew, they started playing more and more
dates outside Liverpool. Brian Epstein pushed as hard as he could
through his contacts in the music business to get them a record deal,
but to no avail. All the big record companies were based in London and
their A&R managers seemed to prefer signing groups nearer to home
rather than new bands from the provinces.

Brian did manage to secure a recording test with Decca Records in
London for New Year's Day 1962. But the Beatles had driven down from
Liverpool overnight on New Year's Eve and after a drink too many were
in no condition to perform at their best. They recorded fifteen songs
but the chief A&R man, Dick Rowe, famously decided to sign a London
group, Brian Poole and the Tremeloes, instead.

Brian eventually secured an audition with Parlophone Records. The
audition went well and the A&R manager, George Martin, asked them
to rehearse more material for a further audition. On their return they
played some of their own songs for George and "Love Me Do" was select-
ed as their first single, released on Friday 5th October 1963. The Beatles
performed their debut single at the Cavern that Sunday.

Due to lack of promotion, the record peaked at No. 17 in the charts,
hardly a smash hit. Their popularity grew and when their second record,
"Please Please Me," was released fans all over the country propelled it to
the top of the charts.

I was just about to leave our house on the afternoon of 3rd August
1963 when I spotted the Beatles arriving at the Harrisons' house in

Gerry and the Pacemakers
(photo Courtesy Les Chadwick Peter Kaye Photography)

George's car, a racing green Jaguar with the licence plate 28 PXX. In their pink shirts, brown suede waistcoats and dark trousers, they leapt out of the car and ran into the house.

I couldn't wait to get down to the Cavern to see them play again and I made sure I was there well before Cavern opened at 7 p.m. I met Sue in town at 5 p.m. and we joined the queue outside the Cavern. It was wise to get there there early, because by the time the doors finally opened the queue stretched all the way down Mathew Street. Little did we know this would be the last time we would see the Beatles at the Cavern.

The club was overflowing, we stood packed like sardines but still managed to drum a beat with our feet and hands. From the back of the crowd we could see the Beatles on stage in the same outfits I had seen them in a few hours earlier.

It was the most incredible experience to hear them playing their number one hit, Please Please Me, after following them on their journey to stardom. Their last performance at the Cavern was filmed. The acoustics were unbelievable, probably the best anywhere.

The memorable night was edged with tears. We had mixed feelings about the Beatles moving on. We were thrilled they had found fame but at the same time couldn't help feeling sad that we had lost them to the rest of the world. After all, they were our Beatles.

Of course, not even the loss of our favourite band could stop Sue and me going to the Cavern, which still pulsated with the sound of brilliant Liverpool groups, all hoping to jump on the bandwagon. We would see several fabulous groups in one night, like Gerry & the Pacemakers, the Merseybeats, Billy J Kramer, the Searchers. the Iveys, the Undertakers, the Escorts, the Big Three, Faron's Flamingos, the Road Runners and many more.

Each night after the Cavern had closed Sue and I would run down to the Pier Head to catch the last bus home. I can remember one night when the Beatles were No. 1 in the charts with "She Loves You." The top deck of the bus was full and suddenly somebody started to sing "She Loves You, Yeah, Yeah, Yeah." Everybody joined in. We sang the whole song several times and were still singing half an hour later when the bus reached the terminus by the English Rose Pub in Macket's Lane.

The Beatles had left Liverpool but the Cavern continued to thrive as a live music venue. Ray McFall installed the latest public address system and brought in partners to set up and operate Liverpool's first professional recording studio in the adjoining cellar at No. 8.

In January 1964 Ray decided to enlarge the Cavern stage to accommodate the larger quantities of amplification equipment rock groups were now using. He had the bright idea of cutting up the old stage into

FROM

THE CAVERN - LIVERPOOL

"The Birthplace of THE BEATLES"

COMES THIS GENUINE PIECE OF THE

CAVERN CLUB STAGE ON WHICH

THE BEATLES

PERFORMED 292 TIMES DURING THE PERIOD

1961 TO 1963

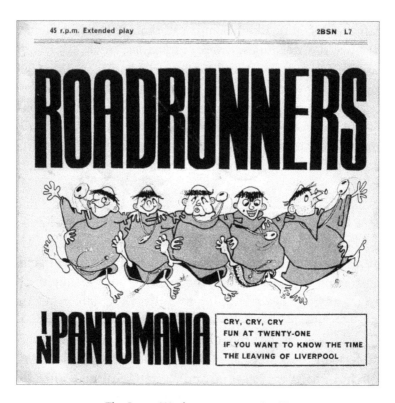

The Panto Week commemorative EP

small pieces and selling each one for five shillings (25p) with proceeds going to Oxfam, a leading British famine relief charity.

The Cavern's management held a cocktail party on 27th April 1964 to mark the opening of their new suite of offices on the ground floor of No. 8 Mathew Street. At the entrance was a reception office with a telephonist/receptionist. The four private offices were occupied by Cavern Artistes Ltd. (Bob Wooler and Doug Evans), Cavern Sound Ltd. (Nigel Greenberg and Peter Hepworth), Cavern Club Ltd. (Bob McGrae), and Ray McFall's secretary (Ann Waugh).

Local businesses frequently approached Ray to ask if they could rent space to trade in the Cavern and gain exposure to the hundreds of captive customers. On Friday 6th November 1964 Tony Rubin, a local entrepreneur, opened a record shop called Pop Record Inn.

A hairdressing salon called Romanoff's also opened in the Cavern and as an opening gimmick they offered free haircuts.

Liverpool, then a vibrant and exciting city in the Swinging Sixties, has always produced unusual talent, not just musical but also dramatic, medical, artistic, scientific and entrepreneurial.

The Cavern Sound partners got a taste of just how innovative Scousers could be when they got involved in a charity fund-raising stunt organised by Liverpool University students in 1965.

During Panto week thousands of students in fancy dress flocked to the city centre with buckets, collecting donations from shoppers and shopkeepers and selling their publication, *Pantosphinx*. There was lots of light-hearted fun – like kidnapping the pharmacist from Boots Chemists and holding him for ransom.

While calling at the Cavern to sell advertising space in their magazine, students asked how much it would cost to produce a commemorative record to be sold for Panto week. Nigel and Peter made a deal with them to produce an EP disc at the studio with two music tracks by the popular local group the Roadrunners and two satirical sketches performed by undergraduates.

The first pressing was 5,000 copies, made by Qualiton Records in South Wales. The students were very pleased with the product and within a couple of weeks had almost sold out. At another meeting in the studio office, Nigel and Peter suggested they should order another 5,000 EPs, but the students hesitated, not wanting to be stuck with un-sold copies.

Quite coincidentally, a young reporter from Mercury Press, a leading Liverpool press agency, was in the office at the time. He "inadvertently and accidentally" overheard the negotiations. After the students left to consider the offer, the reporter approached Cavern Sound with a propo-sition to ensure that all 5,000 records would sell. His idea was to run a story in the tabloid press with a photograph of a teenage girl standing outside NEMS record store in Whitechapel. She was to hold up a copy of the disc, supposedly just bought at the shop, claiming she had discov-ered an unauthorised track not listed on the sleeve when she heard it in the listening booth. The track, titled "My Husband and I," was somewhat disrespectful to the Royal Family and quite risqué.

The hope was that record stores would be inundated with kids hoping to buy the unofficial version. The students enthusiastically embraced the idea and ordered another 5,000 copies. Cavern Sound hastily arranged for the students to write and record a suitable track

Caricatures of the Beatles signed by Bob Wooler and Alan Williams
(courtesy Nigel Greenberg)

and Nigel and Peter drove through the night to South Wales, where Qualiton staff were waiting to press the revised discs.

A young girl was duly photographed outside NEMS holding a copy of the EP. The story appeared in the tabloid press the next day and also in the *Liverpool Echo*. The result was exactly as predicted – the record sold out within days, much to everyone's delight. Well, almost everyone.

Academic eyebrows were immediately raised, and the Cavern Sound directors were hauled before the Vice Chancellor of Liverpool University for allowing their good name to be besmirched with such a distasteful episode. They had to hand over the few remaining unofficial copies and sign an undertaking absolving the University of any responsibility, should the Royal Family decide to take any further action.

The young reporter from Mercury Press Agency was actually Wally Scott, who went on to become a well-known presenter on Radio Merseyside with his cohort Billy Butler. Wally's boss, who had approved the scheme and sold the story to the tabloids, was Terry Smith who went on to found Radio City and Beatle City. He also became a director of Liverpool Football Club.

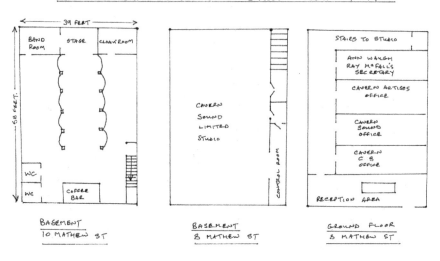

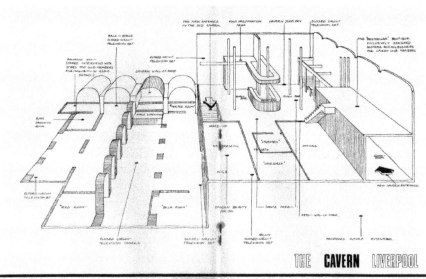

Cavern floor plan before and after remodeling

Damp, Dust and Dead Pigeons

After the meteoric rise to fame of the Beatles, the Cavern and other city clubs continued to pulsate to the new beat. But nowhere could hold a candle to the Cavern. And now here we were barely a year later, facing the challenge of breathing new life into this legendary music venue.

First we had to get the building up to Liverpool Corporation standards so we could re-open. Top priority was connecting to the main drains. The original toilets in the basement were demolished, which involved the unsavoury task of pumping out the cesspit. Modern, smell-free facilities were installed on the ground floor.

Apparently there were underground tunnels beneath the Cavern, where the railwaymen had to come in to work. The stench and overflow from the old cesspit made it impossible for them to work – one factor that had contributed to the closure of the club in February 1966. In keeping with the theme, we named the new toilets Cave Men and Cave Girls.

Next we had to provide a wider access stairway from the ground floor to the club below. The original stone staircase at the entrance to No. 10 could not be widened or used as the main point of entry, so we had a new 8-foot wide staircase constructed at No. 8.

Just inside the new ground-floor street entrance was the pay desk linked by a small passage to a private office behind. A long passageway took you past the cloakroom to the bar, where it opened up into a large area with booth seating. At the back was a large bar directly facing the passageway and to the left were more booths and a small stage for a DJ, with a dance floor in front.

In the small kitchen by the bar staff prepared bar snacks. One of the conditions of having a late drinks licence, albeit occasional at this point, was to have the capability of serving food. Drinks? Who would have thought it? A major change from the alcohol-free days of old.

The kitchen had a door that led into the high-walled brick light-well. When we had first entered the concealed light-well weeks before, the

The original snack bar
(photo courtesy Les Chadwick Peter Kaye Photography)

ground beneath our feet was covered in a carpet of dead pigeons, feathers and pigeon droppings, emitting a foul and stifling smell. Once the birds had flown into the light-well they didn't stand a chance of gaining sufficient height to fly out again, poor things. The space was now thoroughly fumigated and cleared of all offensive refuse.

Dad rewired the electrics, installed disco lights and closed-circuit TV. He designed and built from scratch the new disco with a bar on the ground floor, called the Top Bar, doing all the work himself. He installed all the huge ventilation extractor fans. There were items he couldn't make, like the grill for the bar front. Money was tight and anything he could make he did.

For the major construction work we had to contract with builders and architects to construct the new staircase leading down from the rear of the Top Bar into the club below and to build new toilets on the ground floor.

After close of business at our butcher's shops, I would jump on the bus into town and join Dad at the club to help with anything I could – painting, passing tools, holding wood while he sawed, fetching and carrying, making tea. This was a family affair on a very tight budget

Joe Davey was around from time to time but building was not his forte – but if you needed a wall demolishing Joe was your man. Dad and I were there every night until the early hours, dead on our feet most nights, covered in sawdust and brick dust.

Canon Edwyn Young, Rector of the Parish of Liverpool, would usually call in twice a day to see Dad and sometimes bring him a bite to eat. Sharing a cup of tea with him was a welcome respite from our rigid timetable. Canon Young was based at St Nicholas's Church, known as the sailors' church, with its gilded weathervane in the form of a ship atop its steeple. It dates back to the thirteenth century, when the River Mersey flowed right up to its walls at the Strand on the waterfront.

In front of the church at the Pier Head are the buildings known as the Three Graces. The Royal Liver building with its two magnificent Liver Birds perched atop its twin clock towers. Legend has it that should a virgin ever walk past the Liver building, the birds will fly away. It hasn't happened yet.

The others are the Port of Liverpool Building, which housed the Mersey Docks and Harbour Board, and the Cunard Building, former head office of the famous shipping line. All Cunard Liners, including the Titanic, had been registered with Liverpool as their home port.

Grand Opening   204

of Liverpool's world famous

CAVERN CLUB

SATURDAY 23 JULY 1966

2 p.m. to 5 p.m.   *Admission* **5/-**

A host of show biz personalities will attend, plus T.V., Radio, Film and Press
This you must not miss!

ADMISSION STRICTLY BY TICKET TO MEMBERS ONLY
YOU MAY JOIN ON THE DAY—ANNUAL MEMBERSHIP **10/-**

THE DIRECTORS OF THE CAVERN, LIVERPOOL

request the pleasure of your company at a

RECEPTION

to celebrate the official re-opening of

THE CAVERN CLUB, LIVERPOOL

by

THE PRIME MINISTER

THE RIGHT HONOURABLE J. HAROLD WILSON, O.B.E.,P.C.,M.P.

ON SATURDAY, 23RD JULY, 1966, AT 12 NOON.

R.S.V.P.
To the SECRETARY,
THE CAVERN,   *Guests are kindly*
8-12 MATHEW STREET,   *requested to*
LIVERPOOL.   *endeavour to*
TEL.: 051 236 7881   *attend by 11-30 a.m.*

Dad worked like a Trojan for months to meet the deadline that he and Joe had set to officially re-open the Cavern Club towards the end of July. This gave us three months to comply with all the regulations from the Corporation and the Fire Brigade.

The Cavern Club had never had a drinks licence. Only tea, coffee, Coca Cola, soup and hot dogs were available from the coffee bar at the front of the club. Joe Davey wanted to keep alive the innocent, alcohol-free appeal of the Cavern of its early days.

Dad wasn't so sure. Times had moved on and so had the needs of customers and he thought introducing alcohol would be a step in the right direction. However, for the time being it was placed on the back burner. Once we'd a confirmed reopening date we could apply for an occasional drinks licence for one day.

My mother had contacted Bessie Braddock, the famous local Labour MP at the time and a life-long friend, to ask if she would approach Harold Wilson, the Prime Minister, to officiate at the opening ceremony. Eventually, Bessie contacted my mother to say that the PM had agreed in principal but protocol required that my father submit a written application to his office, which he duly did. The most suitable date in the PM's busy schedule was 23rd July 1966.

Mum took control of the guest list and the invitations for the re-opening. Every celebrity or VIP with any connection to the Cavern Club or Liverpool or Merseyside was invited. They included Brian Epstein and the Beatles, Cilla Black, Gerry and the Pacemakers, Billy J Kramer, the Searchers, the Scaffold, the Spinners, Rex Harrison, Glenda Jackson, Leonard Rossiter, Norman Rossington, Bessie Braddock, Lord Mayor of Liverpool, Ken Dodd, Frankie Vaughan, Lord and Lady Derby and Sir Harry and Lady Pilkington. More than two hundred invitations went out.

The road ahead was long and fraught with problems. With only two weeks to go before the reopening, I remember we had to fit extra extractor fans in the Top Bar to comply with the demands of the local building inspector before the Corporation would allow us to re-open. By working all the hours that God sent and by the skin of our teeth, we made it.

Music Echo published a preview of the reopening.

CAVERN REBORN

by Mike Ledgerwood

Like a phoenix rising from the ashes, Liverpool's famous Cavern Club, birthplace of the Beatles and launching pad of many of the top pop names, re-opens in a blaze of glory.

When Harold Wilson says the magic words at 12.15 p.m. on Saturday, he will mark a new era on Merseyside – an era which started as long ago as 1957 when the dingy disused fruit warehouse in Mathew Street was turned into a jazz cellar. Four years later it became a beat club – and in 1961 at the advent of The Beatles, it switched to rock 'n' roll and became established as the incomparable Cavern Club.

To the Pool the Cavern is and always will be the only place for pop. When the club was forced to close in February this year through financial trouble, Merseyside youth dug their heels in and fought like Trojans.

On the last night they barricaded themselves in the dimly lit cellar and refused to budge. Police were called and the surge of emotional defiance made headlines around the world.

Now all that's past and so is the ill-fated "Save the Cavern Fund," the protest march to the city Town Hall and the sit-down strike by thousands of fans in Mathew Street.

I spent three days in Liverpool last week watching the new Cavern take shape, meeting the pop-minded people responsible for its rebirth and talking to those responsible for its initial success...... the enormous army of fanatical Cavernites.

One thing is obvious. The new venture is destined to be a great success.

The day we had worked so hard to see was upon us. On arrival, each guest would be presented with an official brochure to commemorate the re-opening of the most famous club in the world.

In his inimitable style, Bob Wooler wrote this in the brochure:

THE CAVERN.... A Tomorrow Kind of Club

No. 10 Mathew Street, Liverpool –the most famous Beat music address in the world – a disused warehouse basement and one-time bomb shelter which was opened as the Cavern Club in January 1957 as a jazz cellar. During the course of the next nine years it changed hands and its music policy.

It was to become the most publicised, visited, talked of, written about, photographed, filmed, televised Pop music shrine in the world.

Like a magnet it drew people from all walks of life. When in Liverpool the international 'in' thing was to visit Mathew Street. Rolls Royces rubbed bumpers with battered groups' vans. A case of "if you've never seen the Cavern you've never lived!"

Recorded in the Cavern's VIP visitors' book are the signatures of such celebrities as Arthur Fiedler, Nancy Spain, Dave Clark, Lord Derby, George Martin, Rex Harrison, Chet Atkins, Stanley Baxter, Lionel Bart, Anna Neagle...

The Cavern has a proud history of being the UK's leading launching pad for Pop artists. The show biz luminaries who have achieved world-wide acclaim with the help of the Cavern are legion. It will always be regarded as the Top Cellar that produced so many Top Sellers!

An A to Z of hit parade artistes who during its long history have kept the Cavern in the forefront of popular entertainment venues by appearing at the club would read like a Who's Who of the international Pop scene.

Cilla Black in the early days

The high standards of top quality entertainment established in the past will be maintained in the future. The aim will be to enhance even more the reputation of the club; to make the name the Cavern synonymous with all that is important and exciting in teen appeal happenings.

In the very near future the ultimate popology will be achieved. The combined premises of Nos. 8, 10 and 12 Mathew Street will resemble a kind of subterranean Disneyland Poporium!

A Cavernanza, with dancing, star entertainment, coffee lounge, beauty salons, souvenir shops, boutiques, bowling alley, mini cinema, amusement arcade, closed circuit television, fashion shows and charm school.

A sort of Beatique, specialising in Superpop!

That's the Cavern – a tomorrow kind of club.

Cilla Black said, "I wish I could be there when it re-opens. I've so many happy memories of the Cavern, from working in the cloakroom at lunchtimes to singing with the groups. My favourite song used to be Fever, which I sang with the Fourmost.

"In those days all the groups were going over to Germany, but my mum and dad wouldn't let me. Just one girl among all those lads. I first began to appreciate the Beatles music at the Cavern. At lunchtimes, I used to get five bob (25p) an hour and a free lunch for hanging up the coats at threepence a time. Trouble is I only had an hour for lunch and I either got funny looks from the owner for nipping off early or funny looks from my boss for being back late.

"Yes, I've lots of memories of the Cavern. I'm glad it's being opened again. I wish it every success."

James Duggan, director of Radio Caroline promotions, wrote, "Congratulations to the Cavern, once again on the scene as the club where not only does everything happen but also where it all starts! To prove it, very soon on the Big Twin Sounds of Radio Caroline you'll be able to hear the Cavern's own Radio Show. We at Radio Caroline predict that this Top Pop Show will be No. 1 on everyone's radio popularity charts.

"All through the week on Radio Caroline you'll also be able to hear Cavern newscasts and reports on what's happening and who's on at Liverpool's famous Cavern. Stay tuned to the Big Twin Sounds of Radio Caroline."

Saturday 23rd July 1966 arrived and the world's press was waiting. The red carpet was laid down on Mathew Street and a red ribbon hung across the entrance to the Cavern. Inside, champagne was on ice and canapés were prepared. At 12.15 p.m. the resident of No. 10 Downing Street would metaphorically turn the key to another famous No. 10. Liverpool's famous pop shrine was to be given a new lease of life.

Harold Wilson arriving for the re-opening
(*photo courtesy* Liverpool Echo/*Trinity Mirror*)

The lower end of Mathew Street was packed as far as the eye could see with sightseers, all held back from the Cavern entrance by barriers and a cordon of police officers, while the top of Mathew Street was sealed off from the public awaiting the arrival of the Prime Minister and his party.

Excitement and anticipation quickly overcame our exhaustion when the police opened the barriers for the Lord Mayor's shiny black limousine which pulled to a gentle stop outside the club. Excited chatter burst into a crescendo of cheers and whistles as the chauffer opened the door for Harold Wilson to alight, followed by his wife Mary and his son Giles with the Lord Mayor close behind. The police held the press back as they surrounded the car and converged towards the entrance of the Cavern, all vying for the best shots.

I think Mum was at her happiest at that moment, when all her organizing paid off. She was in her comfort zone dealing with dignitaries. I never once saw her get excited about anything in life and, true to form, she didn't on that day, either.

Dad and I, on the other hand, quietly excited and a little nervous, kept smiling at each other. We remained grounded and looked calm, even with a thousand butterflies in our stomachs. I wasn't sure how Joe and Kath Davey were feeling – their happy smiles were edged with

An unusual line-up on stage at The Cavern on July 25, 1966 - Harold Wilson, Bessie Braddock and Ken Dodd, as Mary Wilson looks on

Prime Minister at the Cavern
(photo Courtesy Liverpool Echo/Trinity Mirror)

apprehension. Joe had asked my Dad to deal with the press for most of the interviews, as he didn't feel comfortable talking to reporters, but he was willing to take centre stage for the photographs.

Dad welcomed the distinguished party and introduced them to Mum, Joe and Kath, and then handed Harold Wilson the scissors to cut the ribbon and to declare the Cavern Club officially open.

Mathew Street was bursting at the seams with press and public. Dignitaries and special guests arrived and were ushered to the club entrance, where they were greeted by Paddy Delaney and other staff who guided them through the Top Bar and down into the Cavern.

Soon the Prime Minister, Bessie Braddock, Dad and Joe Davy wove their way through to the band room and up the two step onto the stage for the speeches. The press pushed to the front of the stage, checking light meters and setting up lights and camera apertures.

This was the moment we'd been waiting for, the culmination of months of blood, sweat and tears. The atmosphere was electric. Deafening cheers echoed through the Cavern tunnels, as Dad went up on stage to thank Harold Wilson and all concerned for making this day so memorable.

But before he could deliver his speech, disaster struck. As all the photographers and cameramen switched on their lights, the electrical system couldn't handle the surge in demand. We were instantly pitched into complete darkness as the main fuses blew. Of course, the microphones went dead, too.

Dad shouted above the chatter. "Is there an electrician in the house?"

From somewhere in the darkness a voice shouted back. "Yes, I know where the electrics are, I'll fix it."

Fortunately for our unknown saviour, the emergency lighting had kicked in, casting a very dim glow that let him see what he was doing while he restored the power. A few minutes later the lights came back on and everybody cheered.

Bessie Braddock said, "The Prime Minister is doing a remarkable job politically. Give him the greatest welcome that Liverpool can."

He read his nicely hand-written speech and went on to pay tribute to the wonderful foreign earning power of the Mersey Beat, a subject obviously very dear to his heart at that time of economic stress.

"It is not a boom we need," he said. "It is determination, the heart to work, liveliness and enjoyment too." He made no apology for speaking in a serious vein, "because I am speaking to serious young people."

He pulled back a small purple velvet curtain on the back wall of the stage to unveil a plaque commemorating the occasion.

HERE'S WISHING A FRESH ERA OF SUCCESS TO
THE CAVERN

THE BEATLES: GERRY AND THE PACEMAKERS: CILLA BLACK:
BILLY J. KRAMER WITH THE DAKOTAS: THE FOURMOST:
THE REMO FOUR: AND BRIAN EPSTEIN

"We have a job to do in Britain, a worthwhile job, so don't be afraid to assert yourselves," he encouraged. "We only got to the top league in our pop culture because our pop groups asserted themselves."

Mum and Kath Davy joined Dad and Joe on the Cavern stage where they presented Harold Wilson with a specially commissioned pipe. Contrary to popular belief, the pipe was not made from a piece of the original Cavern stage but was made by a leading pipe manufacturer from a specially sourced type of wood.

Presentations of commemorative inscribed mugs were given to all the celebrities and dignitaries before everyone made their way back upstairs for a champagne reception in the Top Bar.

Sitting with the Prime Minister's party in one of the booths, Dad got the chance to relax and chat after a hectic day. Mum joined Lord and Lady Derby in another booth. Lord Derby is a cousin of the Queen and one of the region's largest landowners with a family seat at Knowsley Hall near Liverpool that incorporates Knowsley Safari Park in its extensive grounds.

I sat with Sir Harry and Lady Mavis Pilkington and their son Alistair in the next booth. The Pilkington's were members of one of Merseyside's most distinguished industrial families whose

Keeping the Caver|
audience amused witl
their wit are th|
Scaffold. This was thei|
first appearance ever a|
the Cavern. From left t|
right they are: Roge|
McGough, Mike McGea|
and John Gorman

The Scaffold (Mike McGear centre)

predecessors founded Pilkington Bros. glass foundry. In more recent times they developed the float glass process, now used universally to manufacture plate glass windows and car windscreens.

Guests were shown to their seats as waiters wove through the crowd, serving champagne and platters of canapés. Movie star Rex Harrison and his wife, the actress Rachel Roberts, were there along with Norman Rossington, the Liverpool actor who has the distinction of being the only actor to co-star in movies with both the Beatles and Elvis Presley. Comedian Ken Dodd, Jimmy Savile, the now infamous DJ, Louise and Harry Harrison, George's parents, and many others squeezed into the Top Bar to celebrate the occasion.

The Beatles, Brian Epstein, Cilla Black and other celebrities unable to attend all sent telegrams of apology and wished us a wonderful day and every success for the future.

After the Prime Minister's party left and the remaining guests slowly filed out, the barriers were removed from Mathew Street. The Cavern once again opened its doors to the public with three sessions of live music that continued through the day and night until 7 a.m.

SOLOMON   BURKE   ATLANTIC RECORDS

A host of local bands that had developed their stage acts at the Cavern as regular performers for four or five years provided the backbone of the day's entertainment. They included the Hideaways, the Signs, the Escorts, the Chants, Dark Ages, Georgia's Germs, the Excelles, the Strandmen, the Seftons, the Carrolls, the Tremas, the Dollies, the Senates, the Dark Ages, the Rock House Band and the Prowlers.

Nationally famous singers and groups such as Marty Wilde, Georgie Fame, Dave Dee Dozy Beaky Mick & Titch, the Bachelors, the Searchers, Billy J Kramer, the Fourmost and the Merseys also performed during this marathon session.

Internationally famous singers Solomon Burke and Rufus Thomas also appeared. The Scaffold, a singing group that included Mike McGear (Paul McCartney's brother), also entertained the vast audience with their clever and amusing songs. Nationally famous DJs from radio and TV, Jonathan King, Jimmy Savile and Simon Dee, all did a stint at the turntables entertaining the audience between the live bands.

There was much disappointment in the city that none of the Beatles had put in an appearance for the re-opening, but we did all have the pleasure of being entertained by the Pete Best Combo, fronted by Pete Best, the Beatles' original drummer so unceremoniously ejected from the group on the threshold of international stardom.

You could barely move in the club. The Top Bar was full and the Cavern proper down below was bursting at the seams as I descended the newly constructed staircase to the heart of the action. Initially the temperature in the cellar took your breath away but it didn't take long to adjust to that familiar feeling of heat, crowds and music. The only things missing were the condensation and the foul smell of drains.

Bob Wooler with the Escorts

The joint was jumping, visitors were dancing, albeit on the spot. The Hideaways kicked off the entertainment and just minutes into their first song the Cavern was jolted back to life. Its heart was beating again. This is what I had imagined when my Dad said he had the chance to buy the Cavern.

But the day also brought us a nasty surprise. I had returned home late that afternoon with my boyfriend, Alf, to freshen up for the evening. I was about to put my key in the front door lock when I noticed through the glass door panel that matchsticks were sticking up from behind the lock. The door was not locked.

We went in and I ran upstairs to the bedrooms to find that the house had been ransacked. Upturned drawers lay empty on the floor and mattresses were tipped over. Clothes and belongings were strewn everywhere. Every bedroom was the same. We went downstairs to find a similar sight.

There was one cupboard in the rear living room that had been half-emptied, but the rest was as it should have been, indicating that we had disturbed the intruders. Our dog Paddy was shaking and cowering behind the settee. The vet later said that he might have been kicked.

Now I had the impossible task of breaking the news to my Dad without scaring him. God knows, he had enough on his plate.

I rang him at the Cavern and told him we'd had a break-in and the place was a mess but the dog was safe. I asked if there was anything in particular that might be missing. He asked me to check the cupboard in the rear room and look in a shoe box. There should be a canvas bag with the previous day's takings from the butcher's shops which he hadn't had time to bank because of the opening of the club.

I went to the cupboard and frantically searched for the box. To my amazement and our great relief, it was there. We must have disturbed the intruders – there's no way they would have left that behind.

My Dad was so relieved and came home from the club to assess the damage. There was a small amount of money and a few bits of inexpensive jewellery missing from my grandmother's bedroom but that was all.

It was obvious that some low-life opportunist had done his homework and realised we would all be away from the house that day. The local press had carried stories about the club's re-opening for several weeks.

The culprits were never apprehended. Not much had been taken but the psychological trauma was devastating. We felt very uneasy for a long time afterwards.

It was the most astonishing day for us as a family. It was only later that it all sank in. We'd been working so hard that we'd hardly had time to take a breath and contemplate just what we had achieved and of course even as we did so, the day to day logistics of running the most famous music club in the world soon turned our thoughts from reflection to the here and now.

While the mystery of just who it was who had burgled our home would never be solved, the identity of the mystery person who saved Liverpool's big day by turning the lights back on at the Cavern would be solved, but not right away.

Alf and I had stayed home after discovering the break-in instead of returning to the Cavern as intended. My grandmother had come home from the club in a cab around 8 p.m. and we felt she shouldn't be left alone. We were all awake when Mum and Dad got home. Dad stayed for a while as Mum absorbed the shock. I ran Alf home and returned for more tea with Mum and Gran.

Dad returned to the club for the last of the sessions. He wasn't going to miss the climax of that eventful day that he'd managed to pull off with great success.

The place was a mess but we couldn't tidy up completely until after the CID (Coppers in Disguise, as Scousers nicknamed them) had dusted for fingerprints. We were still very much on edge after the burglary. The dog was very nervous, cowering behind the settee every time he heard the front door open. I hardly slept that night. A stranger had been through all my personal possessions and ransacked my room. I had to put the mattress back on my bed, put on fresh sheets and picked up all the clothes strewn around the room.

I heard Dad arrive home around 8.30 a.m. after the marathon session had ended and the revellers had gone home. I was eager to join him and Mum for breakfast to share experiences. Though exhausted by the all-nighter and disheartened by the break-in, he was exhilarated, as we all were, by the successful first night.

We hadn't yet had a chance to exchange two words. It felt like much more than a day since we'd all eagerly awaited the arrival of the Prime Minister. Already it seemed like a distant dream. None of us had had much sleep that night and Dad hadn't had any. The reassuring smell of bacon and eggs wafted in from the kitchen, as Mum prepared breakfast.

Little did I know then that fifteen years later, on a blind date organ-ised by mutual friends, I would not only meet the man who fixed the lights on the opening day of the new Cavern – but three years after that I would marry him. His name was Nigel Greenberg.

Apparently Nigel would also be with us on the Royal Daffodil Ferry on the Mersey when my Dad hosted a party for the launch of Radio Merseyside the following year, but we didn't actually meet until many years later.

I discovered that not only did Nigel know my Dad but had also owned Cavern Sound Ltd., the recording studio installed before the original club was closed by the Corporation. Cavern Sound, a separate company from the Cavern Club, was trading profitably right up till the day the bailiffs moved in.

THE OLD CROWD RETURNS

By Monday 25th July the euphoria of buying and re-opening the Cavern subsided. It was now down to business.

As mentioned, Bob Wooler, Billy Butler and Paddy Delaney, of the original Cavern staff, had asked for their old jobs back and, of course, we were delighted to take them back on board. They had been the backbone of the club, so it made a lot of sense to have the continuity of their familiar faces and their intimate knowledge. They were steeped in Cavern history and loved it as much as I did.

It was an uphill struggle to begin with. Mid-week nights proved to be rather slow but students were given a discount on production of their student union card and we kept regular admission fees very reasonable.

Billy Butler (courtesy Scene 68)

Paddy Delaney (right) with Alf

Anyone could become an official member after paying a membership fee that entitled them to reduced admission for all sessions. We just about broke even on weeknights.

Several live groups appeared every night, introduced on stage by Bob Wooler, the original compere. A DJ played music in the Top Bar, either Billy Butler, former resident DJ, or Bob McGrae, who had previously worked in the Cavern office and had taken the stage name of Robbie Rave or Ron Pimlett. Fred Lloyd, a talented keyboard artist, also played the Hammond organ.

Slowly but surely the numbers increased. I was pleased that one of our first returning members was Baz, who as usual caused havoc among the girls that didn't know him. His real name was Brian Clark but Paul McCartney had christened him Baz. He used to come to the pay desk and talk to Paddy Delaney, standing there with arms folded, chest out, grinning from ear to ear. "All the girls love me, you know," he would remind Paddy, who would reply, "I know they do Baz, they all ask me who's that handsome chap with the fair hair." With that, Baz would grin and belch out one of his loud chuckles and say, "Got to get back to the girls."

Weekends were busy and a very different scene to our sparsely attended midweek sessions. Gradually the Cavern began to resemble the old days, with queues of visitors waiting for the doors to open. The cellar was once again full and reverberating with the unmistakable Mersey Sound.

Bob Wooler and Dad organised all-night sessions on Saturday night which proved to be very successful but very tiring. Clubbers loved the all-night sessions, a chance to escape humdrum everyday life and immerse themselves in the wonderful world of music.

We had to apply for a special licence to cover such events, as the club had still not applied for a full alcohol licence. Bob loved a glass or two of Beaujolais and would try to educate my dad into taking the same tipple when they went for a drink together at The White Star pub at the bottom of Mathew Street. But Dad was a Bacardi and Coke man. They had many a swift social drink whenever they could. The Grapes pub across the street was much closer, but it was frequented by the bands who played the Cavern, so Bob was continually pestered about bookings and for professional advice in general.

Bob had a sharp wit and could be very blunt but you knew exactly where you stood with him. Dad was very similar, with a good sense of humour, very direct with an open countenance. They were good together, both sharing the same love of puns, rhymes and plays on words – and especially the music.

Through the Roy Tempest Organisation, a major London promoter, we had booked Ike and Tina Turner to appear at the club on Saturday 6th August. 1966. However, only their backing group, the Ikettes, turned up. They were a great act and included P. P. Arnold in their line-up. From that day forward we were always suspicious of the authenticity of the acts Roy Tempest provided.

Other stars included Chuck Berry, Lee Dorsey, Long John Baldry, Ben E King, Slade, Gary Walker from the Walker Brothers, Solomon Burke, Rufus Thomas, Edwin Star, Chris Farlowe, the Coasters, Bruce Channel, Bobby Hebb, Bill Haley and the Comets, Jimmy James and the Vagabonds and many more.

Such was the international interest in Liverpool and its music that directors of a London-based production company came up to the city to produce Liverpool A Go Go, which showcased popular local acts performing at the Cavern and on the Royal Iris, one of the ferry boats that plied the Mersey. The film was presented by resident Cavern DJ Bob Wooler.

On a guided tour of the Cavern you finally got the feel of this famous cellar. You knew once and for all where the Beatles blossomed on the famous stage in front of the three arched tunnels full of excited girls and boys. After the film was shown in America, the Hideaways, one of the featured bands, started getting loads of fan mail from the States addressed to them at the Cavern Club.

Around the same time a report in the *Mersey News* described another first for the Club:

> *On Wednesday 10th August 1966, the Cavern's magic casts its spell once again over Liverpool's young people. The Cavern, the place where it all began, and what better place could be chosen for the Northern premier of the beat-music film Gather No Moss than the recognised cradle of beat.*
>
> *The official reopening of the Cavern by the Premier Harold Wilson had nothing on the thundering baptism last week by this new film, the outstanding musical treat of the year.*
>
> *The premier of Gather no Moss, arranged by Scala Cinema manager Jim Walker, was the first film to be shown at the Cavern in all the ten-year history of this famous club.*
>
> *Starring some of the world's top recording artistes performing a unique combination of rock 'n' roll, country and western, folk and traditional blues. Gather no Moss was filmed live at the huge Santa Monica Auditorium, California, during a pop music festival. It has everything: rhythm, movement, speed, wild excitement and the artistry of such great performers as the Rolling Stones, James Brown and the Flames, Chuck*

Berry, the Supremes, the Beach Boys, Gerry and the Pacemakers and Billy J Kramer and the Dakotas.

From the start of the film, when Chuck Berry exploded on to the screen with our dynamic Gerry, the pair performing alternate numbers right through to the end, there was no losing the electric atmosphere.

For any self-respecting beat music fan Gather no Moss is a film which cannot be missed. In fact it is more than a film, it is an experience, and for those who are anti-beat music or just do not understand it, this film is an education.

Gather no Moss opened at the Scala Cinema, Lime Street in Liverpool on Sunday and continues throughout the week.

Chuck Berry was a wonderful musician but not a particularly nice man. He had arranged to meet Bob Wooler outside the Cavern before his performance on 27th February 1967. The club was not yet open and they were waiting in the street for the manager to arrive. Chuck Berry stayed in the back seat of his chauffeur-driven car with his window open an inch or two, talking to Bob while keeping him standing in the pouring rain. He even wanted his money up-front.

Bob wasn't used to this sort of behaviour from artists but knew he had to placate him. I don't know exactly how they managed to get his fee together – my guess is that they rustled it up from petty cash and the bar floats until they could refund it from the night's takings. Bob wrote:

The Beat Goes On at the Cavern. February 27th 1967

The Cavern, a name synonymous with The Beatles, Liverpool and beat, throbbed vibrantly under the sound of Chuck Berry and his guitar. For the 6 foot 1 inch coloured American singer from Missouri, it was his first visit to the Cavern and the verdict? "I have seen some clubs, but this is very good, very nice."

Chuck Berry, probably one of rock's greatest lyricists and stylists but also an odious character! He was a mighty influence on the Beatles and didn't John Lennon once say? "If they hadn't called it rock 'n' roll they'd have called it Chuck Berry," or words to that effect. He influenced all Mersey bands of the early sixties and, of course, the Rolling Stones. He was a pivotal artist in rock 'n' roll history.

The small square stage, backed with egg cartons, was, for the first time, barricaded in, following the previous near-riot at the Saville Theatre, London, but from the stage, the scene for the artistes was unchanged. A dark chasm with a foggy sea of faces, clapping, tapping and swaying to the rhythm.

The dressing room at the side of the stage is a picture of signatures of visiting artistes and admiring fans. In fact, a successful night depends very much on whether the best performers are engaged.

Mr. Berry Casson, the 23-year-old drummer of the Canadians, who have backed Chuck on his European tour, described the Cavern as "unique."

Watching the enthusiasm of the bobbing crowd, it was hard to believe that the Cavern had nearly closed down. Last July two men were responsible for the re-opening. Mr. Joe Davey and Mr. Alf Geoghegan who felt "the kids were entitled to it."

Although the basic appeal of the Cavern has not altered since then, there have been subtle changes.

"People from different towns come now and they are much younger – two of the differences."

Manager and disc jockey Bob Wooler is a fiery enthusiast of the Cavern. He attributed the changes in the place to the fact that "we have lost all the people we have launched and symbols of success are no longer with us as such." He regarded the club as "a tourist attraction" with the emphasis on the "erotic" appeal.

It had been his ambition to invite Chuck Berry over for a long time.

In 1966, Mum and Dad and Joe and Kath were invited to a celebratory evening for the newly crowned Miss World at The Grafton Ballroom in Liverpool. Dad and Joe were introduced to Miss India, Miss Reita Faria from Bombay (now Mumbai). It was a spectacular evening and Miss World was strikingly beautiful.

On a previous occasion when Ben E King arrived early for a performance, he was accompanied by three enormous black female backing singers who, if memory serves, were called the Three Tons of Joy. After completing a short rehearsal and sound check at the club, Bob took

Cavern owners and wives with Miss World

them for a drink at the nearby Yates's Wine Lodge in Basnett Street, where they gave an impromptu performance to the absolute delight of the regulars. Their performance that evening with Ben E King went down a storm.

On Saturday 26th November 1966, Ben E King and the Senates appeared at the Cavern, supported by the Joy Strings, Mommie's Darlings, Signs and Times and the Beechwoods.

Dad and Bob were again moving into the territory of all-night sessions. This would include marathon music nights booked by colleges to raise funds for specific projects. One in particular was for North East Liverpool Technical College in aid of a Sahara expedition. The diverse line-up was a mixture of rock, pop, jazz, Tamla Motown, poetry, disco and even a fashion parade – an amazing cultural medley.

There were over 300 groups playing on the Merseyside scene in 1961. The most successful of all relocated to London when Brian Epstein moved his office and many groups began to disband. However,

Freda Kelly running the fan club

by December 1967 it was very clear there was renewed interest in the scene. New groups were forming. Bob Wooler was so impressed with one group, the Prowlers, that he gave them a residency at the Cavern. "They are one of the best on the scene," he said.

Students at Liverpool schools asked if we could send people to give a lecture on pop music and answer questions. My dad said, "I had no idea until the questions were asked just how concerned youngsters could be over the possibility of becoming a second Beatles.

"Questions such as, 'Where can I take a song I've written, how do I go about forming a group? Don't you think we should have something to fall back on if the group fails?' These questions and many more like them were asked by twelve-year-olds who may well turn out to be the musicians and songwriters of the future. I will now venture to say that the strength, group-wise, is once again getting up to the 1961 stage, which just proves there is still a vast amount of talent emerging on Merseyside."

Mum and Dad's work schedule was taking its toll. Money was tight, as the Cavern devoured every penny that came in. Not only had Dad and Joe to fund the lease but they also had to spend around £4,000 each on building work and refurbishment. That's almost £70,000 each in today's money. No wonder my parents looked grey and overtired.

My boyfriend and I had booked a week's holiday in Majorca and were due to fly out within the next few weeks. I asked Alf if he would mind if we sent Mum and Dad in our place and we could re-book for the following month. He agreed.

After much persuasion Mum and Dad took us up on our offer. Although I was still running the butcher's shops, I could easily manage to take their place at the Cavern for one week in the evenings. We changed the names on the plane tickets (which you could do back then) and I bought them some new clothes on my George Henry Lee store card –shorts, swimwear and short-sleeved shirts for Dad and nightwear, a bathing costume and blouses for Mum.

This was to be Mum and Dad's first trip abroad. Alf and I had been to Majorca the previous year on our first holiday abroad. Foreign travel was becoming very popular after Freddie Laker started flights to Europe from Liverpool Airport. We were blown away by constant sunshine and tall palm trees, eating outdoors at night and late-evening walks without overcoats. Majorca was then unspoilt, un-commercialised and laid back – very different from today.

We gave Mum and Dad our £100 spending money (you could only take £50 each out of the country back then). I told them, "If you don't go anywhere else in Majorca, you must have a night out at Tito's."

Alf and I had seen an amazing performance by Tony Bennett at Tito's the year before. This open-air nightclub was magical, the best on the island. On entering you descended through several floor levels to the stage and dance floor. On each tier were tables set in white linen with floral centrepieces and small table lamps glistening under the night sky.

Mum and Dad did go to Tito's. As they were being ushered to their seats, a voice called, "Alf, what are you doing here?"

Coming towards them was Eddie Amoo from the Chants, a regular Cavern group that happened to be playing at Tito's that week. When just starting up in Liverpool they were often backed by the Beatles.

The Signs

When Eddie told the club owner that my Dad owned the Cavern, they were taken to the best table and treated to the finest champagne. It was the highlight of their holiday – and reminded them of the Cavern's global renown.

Eddie and Chris Amoo finally found fame and fortune many years later as the Real Thing, with many chart successes. In 1976 "You to Me Are Everything" was a UK No. 1 and No. 64 on Billboard's Hot 100 in the USA. They were the most successful black rock/soul band in England during the 1970s. In 2007 writer Paul Du Noyer credited them alongside Deaf School with restoring Liverpool's musical reputation in the 1970s. "Can't Get By Without You" reached No. 2 in the UK singles chart.

When Mum and Dad arrived home, Dad came down the steps of the Laker Airways plane wearing a huge sombrero, at least three feet in diameter, which he'd bought for Billy Butler. Billy duly wore it in his DJ sessions at the Cavern. Shortly afterwards it mysteriously went missing at the Mardi Gras Club after Geno Washington's performance.

Dad told the story of his chance meeting with the Chants in his regular column in *Scene 68*. "It could not have been better. The Chants are one of the hardest working vocal groups in show business and only now, after years of trying, are they being recognised. The Chants and the charts have been a long time coming together but I foresee that very soon.

"Here's another chance for you songwriters," he wrote. "If it's good enough, the Chants will record it. Get that song to me and I'll tell you if it's OK. Don't be your own judge and jury." Dad used to put a large ad in *Scene 68* regularly offering great prizes for his Write a Song Contest. Another column was headed Opportunities. "I am looking for eight groups to feature on a radio programme," he wrote. "Send me details of your group, plus photographs and line up."

He also interviewed Freda Kelly, the famous Beatles Fan Club secretary. When asked to tell readers something about herself, she started with her dogs. "Three lovely little Yorkshire Terriers," she said. "Grania, Wendy and Cherie, three generations of them, daughter, mother, and grandmother."

Freda had been with the Beatles since before Eppy, as she always called Brian. She told Dad about going to the premier of *Yellow Submarine*, describing the Blue Meanies and poor little Mr. Nowhere Man with his fluffy tail, how he knows everything and isn't recognised – until he tells the Beatles what's wrong with the broken submarine engine.

Freda joined the guests for a reception in the basement discotheque beneath the Shaftsbury Hotel, which was fitted out like a submarine. There was a huge slab of ice with baby octopus, crab, shrimp and lobster on top. "D'you know," she said. "I touched one of the fish and it moved, I nearly jumped out of my skin. They were alive and later they were cooked and served with every drink imaginable."

Dad jumped at every opportunity to promote the club and the city. In 1967 he was invited to be a guest judge on the panel of the popular BBC television show *Juke Box Jury*.

In 1966 Dad managed a group called the Signs. They were three lovely respectful young lads in their late teens with superb vocal harmonies – Tony Burns, Pete O'Connell and Dave Kerrigan.

Dad had high hopes for them. As usual, he took them under his wing and they would often sleep over on our front room floor in Greenbank Road after a gig at the Cavern. Dad and Bob Wooler went to see their parents to ask them to witness the signatures on management contracts. Then they set out to find a deal for the band.

Dick Rowe, Decca Records head A&R man, came to the Cavern to hear the Signs perform live. He was so impressed that he told dad he would like to sign the group for a recording contract.

Days later the band was invited to meet Les Reed, the famous song writer, at the Piccadilly Hotel in Manchester, where they were taken to a rehearsal room and each given lyric sheets to follow while Les played the melody on the piano and sang the words to "A Kind of Hush."

After a few hours of practising he was pleased with the way the Signs were singing the song – they even improvised with la la la la la la la la in the bridge. He gave them a reel of tape with somebody singing "Ain't You Got a Heart" on it and he asked the band to learn that as well. He said he was going to see Dick and would be in touch.

A few weeks later Dad and the Signs, excited at the prospect of a record deal, took the train from Liverpool Lime Street for a session at the Decca Studios in London. They were asked to record Ain't you Got a Heart with a 36-piece orchestra directed by Les Reed. The Signs were thrilled to hear their voices on vinyl for the first time.

THE **Cavern** CLUB OF LIVERPOOL

Presents

Friday	25th July	VARIATIONS STORY BOOK
Saturday	26th July	FRANKIE & The COUNTDOWNS DIMENSIONS
Monday	28th July	Party time with THE SCAFFOLD plus BUSINESS
Wednesday	30th July	HIGHFIELDS
Thursday	31st July	CURIOSITY SHOPPE
Friday	1st August	MAGIC LANTERNS MIGHTY JOE YOUNG
Saturday	2nd August	SOUL STAXX MIGHTY JOE YOUNG

It all happens at the Cavern

APPLICATION FOR MEMBERSHIP.
I wish to apply for membership of the Cavern Club. I am over 18.

NAME.....................................
        block letters

ADDRESS..................................
             block letters

SIGNATURE................................

Name of Proposer.........................

Name of Seconder......................... Date....................

Proposer and seconder must be Cavern Club members.

After a couple of weeks Bob Wooler got a call from Decca to say they wanted the lads to come back to re- record Ain't you Got a Heart with a slightly smaller orchestra. When they went back to re-record, it was a different musical director, Ivor Raymonde, who asked the Signs to also record another song called "My Baby Comes to Me." It was all very rushed and they weren't given the chance to learn it properly and only allowed them one take. The Signs weren't happy with it and for a few seconds even forgot the lyrics.

Fast forward a few weeks to the 19th November 1966, when the Signs were invited with Dad to go back down to London to be a contestant on the BBC TV programme, Juke Box Jury. Dad first took the lads to Carnaby Street and bought them smart fashionable outfits to look their best for the show.

The programme was a panel show, hosted by David Jacobs, where judges rated the latest record releases and voted them a hit or a miss. There was also a segment in the show where an unnamed and unseen artist or group performed behind a curtain and the panel of judges would cast their vote.

On the judging panel were Peter Noone from Herman's Hermits, Katy Boyle, the TV presenter, Ron Goodwin, the composer and conductor, and Mia Lewis, a Welsh pop singer. The Signs performed Ain't You Got a Heart and it was voted a hit.

Dad, Bob and the Signs all thought A Kind of Hush was going to be their first single, but Decca insisted the first release should be Ain't You Got a Heart with My Baby Comes to Me as the B side.

At the end of the second session at the Decca studios they were paid off and returned to Liverpool. Dad was suspicious that they had been paid off, and rightly so. They never heard any more about A Kind of Hush until Herman's Hermits released the song, complete with la la la etc., which became an instant worldwide hit.

Strange or not, that Peter Noone was on the panel of judges at *Juke Box Jury* when the Signs performed Ain't You Got a Heart. The Signs were distraught to think that they had been first asked to play A Kind of Hush and felt they had been used. Dad could never listen to that song again without feeling they had been cheated out of it. He thought a lot of The Signs and was convinced they had a great future ahead of them.

Sadly, one of the group members, Dave Kerrigan, passed away on the 28th December 2011. He was in his fifties and was suffering from Alzheimer's. He was such a lovely guy and he will be greatly missed.

I'm pleased to say that in 2016 the remaining two members of the Signs have been rediscovered by a Scottish record company called Vee-Tone. Their 1966 recording of Ain't You Got a Heart has been reissued and was launched on 23rd July 2016 at the 50th anniversary of the Cavern's re-opening.

DRINKS ALL ROUND

On Sunday 12th March 1967 Lee Dorsey appeared at the Cavern wearing a snug white suit. He was a real live wire, supported by Friendly Persuasion, Gale Blues, the Hideaways, the Signs, the Tremors, the Rogues, and the Michael Hey Group. Chris Farlowe appeared on 23rd March, a very gentle and respectful guy who made no demands other than a request for coffee before going on stage.

A Bumper Beat Spectacular organised by the Liverpool College of Building in aid of War on Want was held on 24th May 1967 from 7.30 p.m. to 1 a.m. – five and half hours of dancing, eating and drinking. The terrific line-up included six of the North's top bands: the Cryin' Shames, the Escorts, the Jets, the Signs, the Mad Monks and the Wild Cat Strike.

The Cryin' Shames
(photo courtesy Frankie Connor)

MOST shopgirls would blush if they were asked to show a leg as regularly as pretty Debbie Geoghegan.

But 21-year-old Debbie is always

SHOWING A YESTERDAY..

Mini-skirted Debbie at the abattoir

Hosting the show was Radio Caroline personality Tony Prince. Now we had a licensed bar, admission was restricted to over-18s.

The Cavern had developed beyond all our expectations. With the club buzzing, I continued to manage the butcher's shops, dashing down to see the spectacular shows and famous artists evenings and weekends. I had to cut down on my modelling, a side-line I had enjoyed for several years, but I could still take time off occasionally to do a photo shoot or a show.

It took us about a year to sell the butcher's shops before I could finally join my Dad in the club full time in late 1967. This was far more exciting than butchering and I was eager for my long-awaited fix of the Cavern – and full time really did mean dawn to dusk.

When we took over the club in March 1966 it wasn't licenced for alcohol. Dad's partner, Joe, believed the club should be kept exactly as it was, serving only Coca Cola, hot drinks, soup and hot dogs. He thought the club would somehow lose its innocence if alcohol was introduced.

Dad had always believed a drinks licence was the way to secure the club's long-term future but he always came up against Joe's objections. With business a little slow at the start, Dad managed to convince Joe that they should apply for an occasional licence on weekends to see if this would make any difference. Weekends we were packed but the crowds thinned out during the week.

On weekday evenings, clipboard and pen in hand, Mum surveyed visitors and members. She asked if there was anything we could do to improve their experience at the Cavern, such as booking different types of groups or introducing alcohol.

Times were different now. Cavernites were no longer fifteen-year-olds but mostly eighteen-plus. The overwhelming request was for alcohol. Though they could always get a pass-out and go to the local pub, it would make life a lot easier if the club also served drinks during the week. Dad and Joe finally agreed that it was a question of survival.

Catering facilities had to be upgraded so we could serve serve hot meals, allowing the club to apply for a full licence to serve alcoholic drinks every day (we were closed Mondays). The club got its full licence on Wednesday 9th August 1967, and business improved dramatically.

The bar staff once told me the story of a guy who was drinking rum and blackcurrant at the Top Bar. Each time he came to order another drink he would be a little tipsier than before, his request deteriorating from "rum and black, please" to a slurred "rum and bllrr."

As the bar became busier, he had to wait to be served. The girl standing next to him was in similar shape. Suddenly the two started kissing, which developed into a full-blown snog. When they finally came up for air, she said in a rough Scouse accent. "By the way, what's yer name?"

Some nights after locking up we would get home around 3.30 a.m., have a cup of tea and a bite to eat and race to get to bed before the dreaded milk float clanked its way around the streets and the twitter of the dawn chorus began.

We had moved house from Macket's Lane a few years before and now lived at the edge of a park, fully exposed to the deafening birdsong. Sometimes I was lucky and slept through it, but often I'd just be nodding off and one little bird, usually a robin, would herald the dawn. It was sometimes impossible to sleep, even with a pillow over my head or wearing ear plugs, and we had to open the club at 8.30 to let the cleaners in.

The days would be spent placing brewery orders, stocking the bars, organising bookings, opening the beer delivery hatches for groups to bring in their equipment during the afternoons so they could rehearse on stage. Then we had to check every part of the club for missing light bulbs and take care of routine maintenance.

Before we reopened in July 1966, we had been advertising on Radio Caroline, the pirate radio station. It attracted a huge audience of young listeners, so it was an obvious medium for us. Caroline was an immediate smash hit with young British record buyers, who could now listen at all hours to non-stop pop music.

At the time the commercial-free BBC had an absolute monopoly on radio broadcasting. For years Radio Luxembourg had broadcast paid advertisements but reception in the UK was very patchy and quite often half way through a track the music would fade. The secret lay in being able to broadcast from a location much closer to the UK than mainland Europe.

A young Irishman by the name of Ronan O'Rahilly had the brilliantly simple idea of setting up a radio station on board an old trawler, anchoring it three and a half miles off the Isle of Man and broadcasting to the UK. As British Territorial Waters at that time extended three miles out to sea from the low water mark of the coastline, the operation was outside UK jurisdiction. The British Government, and in particular Harold Wilson the Prime Minister, did everything in their power to close the station down but but for the time being there was nothing they could do.

In inclement weather the DJs couldn't board the tender that normally took them from Ramsey in the Isle of Man across three and a half miles of treacherous waters, often with twenty foot waves. The station needed local land-based recording and production facilities to produce hours of recorded programmes for broadcast when the DJs couldn't get there.

CD cover of Live at the Cavern *from Cavern Sound original recordings*

Caroline had their Liverpool office in Lord Street, above Tru Form Shoes. The sales team, John Wilde and John Seddon, soon learned that production facilities were available a few hundred yards away and Cavern Sound Ltd., in their basement studio next to the Cavern, had started producing programmes and jingles for them in 1965.

Studio co-founder Nigel Greenberg remembers: "We had to observe a strict continuity regime to ensure that none of the DJs mentioned the current weather in the taped sessions, which might bear no resemblance to the weather on the day the tape was broadcast.

"The record companies loved Radio Caroline because frequent and judicious airplay could make a record an instant hit. For example, after continuous and exhaustive airplay on Caroline, She's Not There by the Zombies rapidly raced up the UK pop charts."

Radio Caroline production work took up most of the studio's time until the Cavern club was closed down in February 1966, but the

The Cavern Boutique

studio was soon relocated to nearby basement premises in Eberle Street, renamed Commercial Production Associates, and continued the pre-recorded programming for Radio Caroline.

But after Radio Caroline was closed down on 14th August 1967, it was all over. Nigel laments: "With Radio Caroline as our only regular client, we had committed the cardinal business mistake of having all our eggs in one basket and we had no option but to close the studio for good."

Meanwhile, after we reopened the club that summer of 1966, Kevin Duggan and his French wife, Françoise, who lived in Liverpool, and his brother Jimmy, who ran Radio Caroline North, were regular visitors to the Cavern. As their involvement deepened, they asked Dad if they could open a boutique on the premises.

Dad needed no second bidding and, with his usual energy, flair and commitment, designed and built a boutique over the offices and cloak-room, accessed by a wooden staircase from the Top Bar. It was mutually beneficial – they had a fashion outlet and the rent we charged paid for our advertising on Radio Caroline.

A society friend of theirs, the Hon. Bunty Killearn, sister of Lord Killearn and daughter of the late British ambassador to Egypt during the war, had an interest in the boutique and provided stock from her husband's wholesale fashion business in London's Fulham Road.

They sold way-out fashions in psychedelic colours, extreme and unusual-shaped mini-dresses adorned with beads and applique, and sexy cat-suits that proved to be very popular with Cavern regulars. I did buy some items from the boutique but still got most of my clothes from The Looking Glass boutique in North John Street.

Jimmy Duggan from Radio Caroline in the Cavern Boutique

YOU ARE CORDIALLY INVITED TO JOIN

THE CAVERN PARTY

AND

B.B.C. RADIO MERSEYSIDE

ABOARD THE 'ROYAL DAFFODIL'

at 11-30 a.m.

ON WEDNESDAY, NOVEMBER 22nd, 1967

BOAT SAILS 12 NOON PROMPT   **215**

Fashions had changed dramatically from the pencil skirts and bee-hive hairstyles and the duffel coats and polo-necked sweaters of the early sixties. Now the mini-skirt was in vogue, getting shorter by the day – Dad called them pelmets. Twiggy's face stared out from every magazine and billboard. Hairstyles became shorter as girls switched to the Mary Quant bob. Knee-length boots were available in every colour – I owned two pairs, one bright yellow patent leather and one dusky pink suede.

Psychedelic coloured matching mini-coats and trilby hats featured in the shop windows of Carnaby Street in London. Biba in Kensington Church Street, London, was one of the coolest boutiques, with its limited-edition outfits guaranteed not to be seen twice and an extensive and exciting make-up range.

Biba boutique was a theatrical wonderland set in Cavern Club darkness, more of a boudoir than a boutique. Cilla Black and Cathy McGowan were regular clients.

The Duggans' boutique was a great success until Radio Caroline was forced off the air by the Marine and Broadcasting (Offences) Act 1967. The authorities couldn't prosecute Caroline, as it was based outside British territorial waters, so they made it a criminal offence for

The Klubs on stage with Alf

anyone subject to UK law to supply any product or service to or assist in the operation of a pirate radio station.

It is ironic that Harold Wilson, a modernising Labour Prime Minister, should kill off pirate radio. The same man who had opened the Cavern Club had helped push through the law that killed off the public's favourite radio station.

On 14th August 1967 Radio Caroline ceased broadcasting, the boutique in the Cavern closed and the Duggans left Liverpool. It was a sad day for all of us, as we had enjoyed a good business relationship with Radio Caroline and a close bond with the Duggans.

But three months after we'd lost one radio station we gained another. On 22nd November 1967 the Cavern hosted the launch party of BBC Radio Merseyside on the Mersey ferry, Royal Daffodil. The boat sailed at noon from the Pier Head. Dad was the first person to be interviewed on Radio Merseyside by Keith Macklin.

An icy wind was blowing as we sat shivering on a wooden seat on the ferry's top deck. It was slightly warmer on the enclosed lower deck where Keith and DJ Tony Wolfe played sixties music. Local groups – the Detours, Excelles, Tremors, and King Bees – entertained us with live music, as guests drank and danced to keep warm.

In December 1967 Joe asked my Dad if he would buy out his interest in the Cavern. He had realised it wasn't really for him and his health was deteriorating. This was a bolt out of the blue, as Dad was still struggling to break even and now had to fund the purchase of Joe's shares.

The money from the sale of the butcher's shops wasn't enough. The North Hill Street branch was the only shop sold at a fair price. The Upper Hill Street shop, with an adjoining house, had a compulsory purchase order slapped on it by Liverpool Corporation for building land for new flats and dad received only a portion of the market value.

The third shop, in Frensham Way in Halewood, was leased from a London company and he had to pay to get out of the lease. Consequently it would now take much longer than anticipated to break even. Finally, he and Joe made a deal to complete their transaction over twelve months.

Without a partner and quite skint, Dad now had to put his nose to the grindstone to make the Cavern once more the greatest club on earth.

Celebrities, Tourists and Doormen

The Cavern doors were always open so we could welcome the continuous stream of tourists who wanted to see for themselves this world-famous venue. Usually visitors would ask if they could take something as a souvenir, a beer mat, a letterhead with the Cavern logo on it, anything at all that would mark their visit to the shrine.

Never one to miss an opportunity, Dad instantly saw a chance to establish a niche market selling memorabilia. He started designing a vast range of souvenirs bearing the Cavern logo: pennants, diaries, address books, car stickers, birthday cards, double-sided engraved medallions on metal chains, cuff links, lapel badges, T-shirts, purses and guitar cases – the list was endless.

The original Cavern membership cards issued between 1957 and 1966 were rectangular with the Cavern logo on the front. We introduced new cards in 1966, slightly larger than the originals with the original logo. These were in circulation up to 1970 and no other type of membership card existed.

It has been claimed that medallions engraved on one side only – which were not original – and hanging on leather cords were used as a form of membership for entry to the Cavern in the sixties. This was definitely not the case. They may have been used after 1970 after we sold the Cavern, but certainly not in the sixties.

While attending St. Francis Xavier's College in his youth, Dad had won first prize at least five years in a row, which in turn had earned him a lifetime scholarship to Liverpool Art College. But he never went because his parents couldn't afford the materials he needed. The irony is that when he could afford to develop his artistic talent he didn't have the time.

Designing souvenirs was easy for him. He'd already done the artwork for the commemorative mugs presented to celebrities at the club's re-opening and he was eager to meet this new challenge.

Cavern souvenirs

The next step was to open a souvenir shop. An office next to the cloakroom by the street entrance was ideal, so we remodelled the area, removing the office wall to build a large display space. Smaller items were on view beneath a large glass display counter, while larger items like T-shirts and guitar cases were displayed on the shop walls. A metal roller shutter secured the stock when the shop was closed.

The souvenir shop did very good business. Smaller lightweight items such as address books, purses, pennants, greeting cards, cufflinks, medallions and T-shirts were very popular with overseas visitors. Guitar cases, mugs and photo albums weren't quite as easy to carry home, but people still stocked up on larger items. All day long tourists from near and far streamed through.

Dad was proved right about memorabilia. Today an enormous quantity of merchandise is sold daily at the new Cavern Club, as well as the Beatles Shop at the bottom of Mathew Street, the gift shop in North John Street and the Beatles Story at the Albert Dock.

On Wednesday night 1st November 1967 Mum was at the club's pay desk. With their latest record riding high in the charts, the Who had just played to a sell-out audience at Liverpool's Empire Theatre. They arrived at the club unannounced and Paddy Delaney, always on duty at the main door, proudly introduced them to Mum.

"The Who, Mrs Geoghegan." And of course Paddy was ready to let them through immediately.

"Who are they, Paddy?" Mum asked.

"They are the Who, Mrs Geoghegan."

"Yes I heard you, but who are they? Are they members?"

Paddy leaned over to the pay desk.

"You're just going to have trust me on this one, Mrs Geoghegan."

"Oh, all right then," was her reply.

A somewhat embarrassed but very relieved Paddy ushered the Who into the club free of charge. If only I had been on the desk instead of her! But then we would never have had all the laughs over the years. Every time we hear the Who mentioned we can't help saying, "The Who, Mrs Geoghegan!"

The Scaffold appeared regularly every Monday night. A notice read: "WE WANT TO BE HAPPY AGAIN (and why not) so, EVERY MONDAY AT THE CAVERN we invite all nice singers, swell players, great reciters,

The Scaffold

good sausage eaters, to come along and help the entertainment. Please let's all join hands and have ourselves a lovely time all round on me. ('What's that supposed to mean? I don't know, I think you're right about him')." It was signed: JOHN GORMAN p.p. Scaffold

Now the butcher's shops had been sold, I was working full-time in the club during the day and took over from Mum on the pay desk at night. Dealing with celebrities was just part of the job.

One such was the (now infamous) late Jimmy Savile. Most Saturday nights Dave Eager would drive Jimmy's Rolls Royce into the Fruit Exchange loading bay across from the Cavern entrance and park for the night. Dave would join me for a chat while Jimmy went down into the Cavern to soak up the atmosphere. We never saw him through the evening until it was time to leave, when he would emerge always alone, head bowed, never very talkative. He would gesture to Dave and they would disappear into the night in his Rolls. We never ever saw him leave with anyone.

Celebrities would often arrive unannounced. Mick McManus, the famous wrestler, called in one night and stood chatting to Paddy and me before going into the club to soak up the sounds. He was such a lovely man, gentle and laid back, the complete opposite of the guy we were used to seeing in the wrestling ring.

Pop singer Alvin Stardust walked in one night, very striking with his mop of dark curly hair. I remembered him from previous years in a different guise as Shane Fenton with fair hair. Paddy and I had a great night chatting to him about his career and his past personae. We reminisced about shows at the Empire Theatre where he appeared as Shane Fenton with Marty Wilde and Eden Kane. He went on to marry

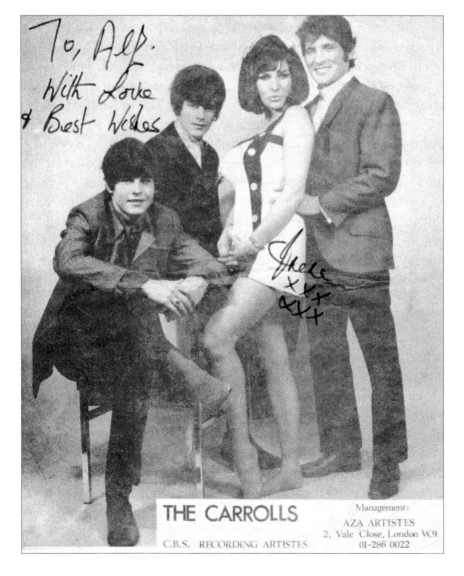

THE CARROLLS

C.B.S. RECORDING ARTISTES

Management:
AZA ARTISTES
2, Vale Close, London W.9.
01-286 0022

Lisa Goddard, the blonde beauty and famous actress from the television series *Yes Honestly*.

Groups would often rehearse in the Top Bar during the day. One of the regulars was the Carrolls, consisting of lead singer Irene Carroll and her three brothers. Her husband, Len Wady, managed the group, which had a great sound. Irene later became famous as Faith Brown and went on to be a wonderful impressionist and latterly a first-class actress.

They rehearsed several numbers each day, including what seemed to be their favourite, "San Francisco (Be sure to wear some flowers in your hair)," by now a UK number one hit. To this day I can't hear that song without thinking of Irene at the Cavern. I still catch up with her when she's in Liverpool doing a charity show or acting. The last time was in her dressing room at the Liverpool Empire where she had the lead role of Norma Desmond in Andrew Lloyd Webber's *Sunset Boulevard*.

Groups were rehearsing all day either in the top bar, or on the Cavern stage, or sometimes both. The Hideaways, the Iveys, the Curiosity Shoppe and the Klubs were all regulars. Dad managed the Klubs, the Curiosity Shoppe and the Signs. He was quite a prolific songwriter and the groups he managed often sang his "If I were a Judge," "Living Today," "Psychedelic Sarah" and "Mrs Penny," a song he wrote for The Scaffold. My favourite was a ballad he wrote especially for me called, "Little Girl (Bells of Christmas)."

The Klubs played one Saturday afternoon at a fund-raising event in St. Nicholas's Church at the Pier Head, where the Cavern laid on a buffet. It seemed incongruous and a little embarrassing to hear them belting out their hard rock in a place of worship. Canon Edwin Young, the Rector, loved it, suggesting that it was their interpretation of giving thanks to God for their talent.

Dad had secured a contract – or so he thought – for the Klubs to do a three-month tour of Northern French venues, including Paris, Lyon and Poitiers. The booking was arranged with the owner of a beat club in Dieppe, so their first stop was the promoter's Cabriolle Club. Dad travelled with them and they stayed in a boarding house in Puis outside Dieppe. After settling the boys in with their first gig, Dad returned home.

Three weeks later he got a phone call from the very desperate band members, pleading, "Come and get us out of this hell hole, Alf, we can't

Faith Brown, formerly Irene Carroll (right) with Debbie

take any more." What should have been a week at each venue turned out to be one never-ending gig in the Cabriolle Club.

Dad was on the next ferry to Dieppe to rescue the band. He spent a few nights there before they all returned to Liverpool. A fairly recent conversation with a couple of group members leads me to believe they painted the town red before they left.

Dad was very friendly with Bill Collins, manager of the Iveys and also father of Lewis Collins, who became famous as Bodie in the hit TV series *The Professionals*. Dad would give the Iveys regular gigs at the Cavern. A popular Welsh band based in London, they had a great sound but always seemed strapped for cash, even though they were the first group signed by the Beatles' Apple Records.

Dad would frequently bring them home for a meal and a bed for the night. I would come home from the club to find them sitting cross-legged in our front room, eating fish and chips out of a newspaper. I use the term "bed for the night" loosely as they always kipped in our front room on the settee, in armchairs and on the floor.

One particular night they brought another guy with them when they showed up at bedtime. It happened to be Kris Kristofferson. We didn't know who he was, just another friend of theirs who needed feeding, one more in a long line of musicians that traipsed through our house at all hours. I always steadfastly refused to give up my bed for anybody.

Paddy Delaney, our head doorman, was a gentle giant but when called upon he could certainly deliver the muscle. One New Year's Eve all the visitors and most of the staff had gone home, except four of the doormen, Paddy, Dad and me.

Suddenly one of the doormen went berserk, racing through the Top Bar, hurling chairs and tables as he fought off the other doormen. Then he ran down the corridor and began smashing up one of the offices. The other three doormen had done their level best to restrain this guy but he was like somebody possessed. Dad found Paddy, who was checking for stragglers before we locked up.

Meanwhile, I made a quick retreat to the Ladies and peeped around the door. I came out to watch as Paddy ran into the office where this maniac was causing havoc, throwing chairs and tipping up filing cabinets and desks.

The Iveys, later Badfinger

"All right lads, leave him to me," Paddy told the others as he shut the office door.

The culprit took a run at Paddy and with one mighty punch Paddy sent him flying across the office. He hit the wall, slid down and landed in a heap on the floor.

Paddy dusted off his hands, opened the door and shouted, "OK, lads, he's all yours, get him out of here!"

I'd never seen anything like it. He was so matter of fact about the whole thing, which was probably down to his training in the Irish Guards. The other lads dragged the offender out into the street and propped him up against a wall to sober up, as we locked up the club and went home.

Happy New Year!

Over the years we employed many doormen, an essential part of club life. Most of the doormen under the direction of the legendary Paddy handled the crowds with diplomacy, tact and a smile. They had to control an entrance thronged by five or six hundred excited teenagers waiting to see a favourite group play. Tempers sometimes frayed when those near the back of the queue realised they were not going to get in, but generally there were few problems.

Paddy was first recruited as head doorman in 1959, when Ray McFall took over the Cavern, and remained a permanent fixture until it closed in 1973. He always called my Dad "Chief." He was courteous, kind, very astute, had a wonderful sense of humour and could sniff out somebody dodgy from a mile away.

Very proud of his position at the Cavern, he got upset if anyone referred to him as a bouncer. "Doormen are diplomats, bouncers are not," he would retort. Most visitors were suitably impressed by the sight of the gentle giant in evening dress giving everybody the once-over before they were allowed to descend into the club.

On Guy Fawkes Night in 1963, the Rolling Stones were playing at the Cavern, and Sue and I waited patiently in line for hours. There were just two people in front of us when Paddy put his arm across the entrance and said, "Sorry folks, we're full up, we can't take any more." Sue and I were very disappointed, but could console ourselves that we had seen them in Jersey months before.

I reminded Paddy of this when he came to the Cavern four years later to ask us for his old job back. "If I'd have known you were going to be my future boss, of course I would have let you in," he laughed.

A frustrated performer himself, Paddy would sometimes do his Al Jolson tribute on the Cavern stage. He would go down on one knee and give a powerful performance of "Mammy," to our delight. But he was a family man first and a celebrity second. He thought the world of his wife, Margaret, and their six children.

The last time I saw him was at Doug Evans's funeral. Doug was the Cavern office manager in the early sixties and had also been a director of Cavern Artistes Ltd. with Bob Wooler. Paddy had lost his beloved Margaret and was going home to an empty house. We offered to take him and Ray McFall for a meal at Greenhill's Pub in Allerton, where we ended a poignant day of mainly happy memories.

One of the doormen at the Cavern was a guy called Joseph Keatley, known to everyone as Beech, who had worked the door at many city centre clubs, including the Iron Door, the Cabaret Club and the Tower Ballroom in New Brighton. He was a former heavyweight boxer and had sparred with some of the country's top prize-fighters.

He'd inherited the nickname Beech from his merchant seaman father, John, who was known as the Beach Boy after once missing his ship in New York and having to wait on a sandbank for the next ship home.

I had always found Beech to be pleasant, quiet natured, respectful and not a bit confrontational. He didn't turn up for work one evening in 1968 and word gradually filtered through the grape vine that he had been run down by one of Liverpool's most notorious gangsters, Eddie Palmer. Beech survived but spent weeks in hospital recovering from two broken legs.

Months later he came to see us at the Cavern, struggling to walk with the aid of two crutches. He told Paddy that he knew it was Eddie Palmer who had deliberately run him over. "The bastard won't get away with this. I'll have him for what he's done to me."

Ten years later Beech seized an opportunity to reap his revenge. One night in the car park of the Peel Labour Club in Dingle, he watched as Palmer got into a taxi with two women. When Palmer made an insult-

Rocky Seddon (left) with Tom Jones and friend at Tom's ranch

ing remark about Beech's ex, Beech opened the car door and lunged at him with a knife, intending to stab him in the arm. But Palmer raised his arm to fend off the blow and the knife went into his chest. Eddie Palmer died on the way to hospital.

Beech was arrested and tried for murder but a petition was handed to the court in his support. Many people were glad to see the back of Palmer. At the trial the prosecutor said Palmer was the most feared man in Liverpool. Beech was cleared of murder, convicted of manslaughter and jailed for three years.

As he was being taken down to the cells, the Judge said, "Good luck," implying that Beech had done the local population a great favour. On the day of Eddie Palmer's funeral, pubs held celebration parties and the city of Liverpool breathed a collective sigh of relief.

Another regular doorman was Rocky Seddon, who had to go part-time after his first year with us when he landed a job as Tom Jones's bodyguard. For the six months of the year when Tom was touring Rocky would be gone and we kept his job open until he returned.

He used to entertain Paddy and me with stories of his time touring with Tom and he brought me a signed photograph of him with Tom at the Jones ranch in America. One strange confession I always remember was that Rocky told me he liked to sleep in black silk sheets. This was not the sort of thing you would expect of a one-time boxer from Liverpool – it could only have come from Tom Jones's dude ranch.

It should be mentioned that Paddy Delaney and Billy Butler, the Cavern DJs, were staunch Everton supporters and no doubt Billy still is. Though a staunch Liverpool supporter, Dad would pray for Everton to win their Saturday football matches, otherwise Paddy would be so miserable that he would turn away far too many people at the door – and our takings would plunge. Even then, people who did manage to get in would have to put up with a miserable Billy.

Billy Butler was as much a part of the Cavern as Paddy Delaney and Bob Wooler. He was a natural and is still a well-respected presenter on BBC Radio Merseyside.

Bob Wooler's contribution to the Mersey Beat scene was immense and the scene likely would not have happened without his efforts at the Cavern. A very articulate man with a sharp, sardonic wit, he had a smooth silky voice to introduce performances with the words, "Hi there, all you Cave Dwellers. Welcome to the best of Cellars."

Born Frederick James Wooler in January 1926, he always claimed his birth year was 1932. While working as a railway clerk at Garston Docks, Bob had taken his tape recorder to the office Christmas party in 1956 to record a skiffle group formed by two lads from another department. Impressed with the results, they asked Bob if he could get them any bookings.

Soon he was finding bookings for other groups as well and started compering lunchtime sessions at the Cavern, where rock 'n' roll groups were now allowed at what had been until recently a jazz-only club. In 1960 he gave up his job at Garston Docks for full-time employment at the Cavern, where he stayed for the next seven years.

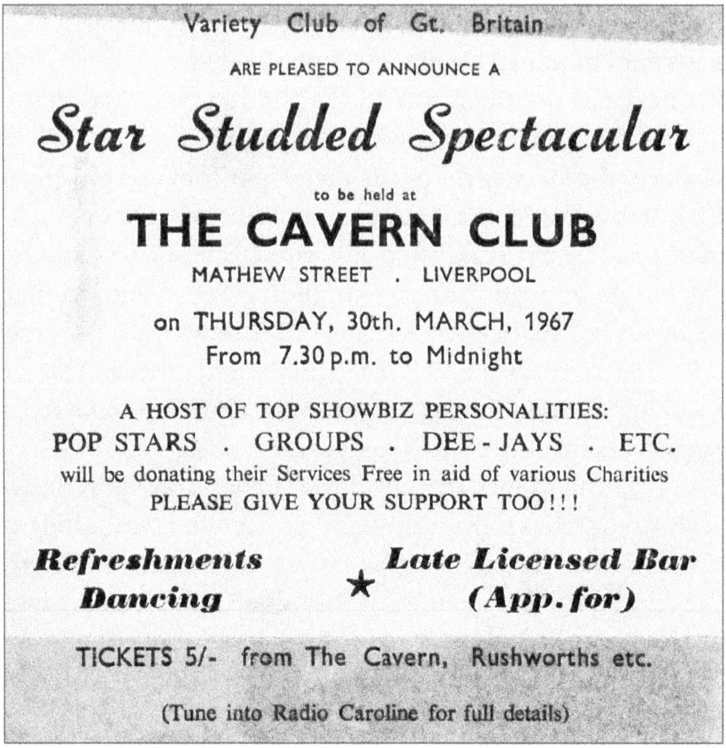

Variety Club of Gt. Britain

ARE PLEASED TO ANNOUNCE A

Star Studded Spectacular

to be held at

THE CAVERN CLUB

MATHEW STREET . LIVERPOOL

on THURSDAY, 30th. MARCH, 1967
From 7.30 p.m. to Midnight

A HOST OF TOP SHOWBIZ PERSONALITIES:
POP STARS . GROUPS . DEE - JAYS . ETC.
will be donating their Services Free in aid of various Charities
PLEASE GIVE YOUR SUPPORT TOO ! ! !

Refreshments   **Late Licensed Bar**
Dancing   ★   **(App. for)**

TICKETS 5/- from The Cavern, Rushworths etc.

(Tune into Radio Caroline for full details)

The Cavern was starting to look like its old self again. The club was full every weekend and almost full weeknights. We regularly had celebrities turning up on our doorstep out of the blue. You never knew who was going to call in next.

Thursday 30th March 1967 Spike Milligan visited and danced the night away to the early hours. He was appearing in *The Bed Sitting Room* at Liverpool's Royal Court Theatre and was a guest at a charity show at the club. Other guests included cast members from Spike's play, Valentine Dyall, Bill Kerr and Denise Stafford.

Organised by the Variety Club of Great Britain in conjunction with the Cavern, the show featured a number of Liverpool beat groups, including an Army group from Cyprus called The Kingtones and an appearance of the celebrated Scaffold – John Gorman, Roger McGough and Mike McGear.

Spike said, "This is the fourth time I have been to Liverpool but I have never visited the Cavern. I have always wanted to look it up and now that I have, it completely lives up to my expectations. I can't say that I am too struck on this beat type of music as I am very fond of modern jazz."

Long after the groups had finished playing Spike, Dad and I were sitting cross-legged on large beanbag cushions on the floor of the then-redundant Cavern boutique, totally engrossed in a conversation about spiritualism. Behind Spike's wild and unruly sense of humour lay a deep-thinking mind and a sensitive soul. He only drank Coke as the three of us talked for hours.

Spike Milligan dances the night away

The bands were packing them in at the Cavern. Here's the May line-up listed by Alf in *Scene 68*:

> *Groups Appearing at the Cavern*
>
> *Friday May 3rd 1968, Thyme & Motion*
>
> *Sat May 4th Marvin Young Sound Package*
>
> *Wed May 8th The Liverpool Scene.*
>
> *Fri May 10th Tremas*
>
> *Sat May 11th Baltimore Switch.*
>
> *Sat May 18th Famous Watson Brown*
>
> *Perfumed Garden.*
>
> *Sat 25th May Kasper's Engine.*
>
> *Fantastic nights are planned for the Cavern.*
>
> *Admission Friday 4/- Saturday 5/- 8 till 2 a.m.*

Things didn't always go as planned. Alf had to apologise in *Scene 68* for no-shows by Bill Haley and the Comets and Kasper's Engine – though Bill Haley did play another date.

A frantic fortnight at the Cavern in June 1968

First we suffer the non-appearance of Bill Haley and the Comets through a contract misunderstanding. Fortunately the crowd of over 500 rock-happy patrons took the news (and cash refund) very well. The following Saturday there occurred an example of how success (even a limited quantity) can affect a group's ego.

Kasper's Engine arrived at the Cavern to find that the entrance was blocked by a vehicle. Many frantic messages speed through the club to find the owner – with success – so the car is moved, but where are Kasper's Engine? They have apparently decided that they are too big to be kept waiting and so have sped silently away into the night.

It's 12 a.m. the Cavern is packed out but one thing is missing – the group, a dilemma faced by too many club owners these days. Fortunately, The Seftons and The Colour were on hand and offered to fill the gap. We would like to place our appreciation to them and their professionalism on record in Scene 68. Thanks Lads.

Bruce Channel

Billy Butler in *Scene 68*:

Bruce Channel appeared at the Cavern, Wed September 25th 1968. This was his second appearance at the club. The first appearance was in 1961 with his hit, Hey Baby, and this time with Keep On.

In fact Bruce Channel is star material in every sense of the word. His backing group, Dr. Marigold's Prescription, was a tonic for any patient in the doldrums. If you are good at the Cavern we hear all about it from the members before they leave. So Dr. Marigold's Prescription shoots up to join the Cavern's favourite groups after only one performance. We shall have them back soon.

PAUL RETURNS

It was 25th October 1968 and I had paid my usual Friday visit to the hairdressers and arrived at the club mid-morning to start work. Dad was stocking the Top Bar when I arrived.

"We've had a visitor," he said.

"Who was it?" I asked.

"Paul McCartney," he said.

"So I've missed him?" To say I was disappointed doesn't come close.

"Don't worry he's coming back," Dad assured me. "You finish stocking the bar and put some champagne on ice, I'm going to the photography shop to buy a camera."

Dad walked across North John Street to Photo Optics in Dale Street. He had to spin the photographer a yarn that he wanted to take photographs of a group in the club and asked if he'd he come over and set up the camera so he wouldn't have to do anything but take photos.

Paul had just walked into the club out of the blue while Dad was stocking the Top Bar ready for the evening.

Recognising him instantly, Dad held out his hand.

"Hi, Alf Geoghegan, the Cavern."

Paul shook his hand and replied, "Hi, Paul McCartney, the Cavern."

"I'm going over to the Wirral to deliver a record player to Ruth, my stepsister, and I'd like to come back later. I've got my girlfriend in the car and I'd like to show her the Cavern, on one condition – you don't tell the press."

"You've got it," Dad said. "Would you mind if we took some photographs?"

"No that's fine, I'll be back in an about an hour."

The Hideaways were rehearsing in the Top Bar at the time and couldn't believe their eyes when Paul walked in unannounced. I continued to stock the bar. Dad returned about half an hour later with the photographer, who set the shutter speed and lens aperture on the newly purchased Yashica camera.

Debbie and Paul McCartney (photo © Tracks Ltd.)

We were all on tenterhooks waiting for Paul to return with his new girlfriend, Linda Eastman. The champagne was on ice and we were ready. Would he come back or would he have a change of heart?

True to his word a couple of hours later in walked Paul with Linda.

He wore a very long black great coat to the floor over a white open necked shirt and dark trousers and his dark hair was long. She was blonde, tall and wore a pale pink cardigan buttoned up to the neck and a pair of tight black trousers that looped under the foot. She wore no make-up and was very natural looking.

By now there were only five of us in the Top Bar, Paddy Delaney, Dad and I, and Paul and Linda, though Billy Butler was around somewhere.

Dad locked the main door to prevent any visitors wandering in. We gathered by the bar where Dad offered them a drink and proceeded to open the champagne.

"I'll do that," Linda said. "I'm a good bartender." She took over and served the champagne.

Dad made a toast: "To Paul and the Cavern."

He asked Paul again if he could take some photographs and was about to pick up the camera, when Linda said, "I'll do that, I'm a good photographer."

She picked up the camera and after altering all the settings started to take the shots. Dad was afraid she'd messed up the camera settings.

We chatted for a good half hour, reminiscing about the Beatles' early days, Liverpool and the Cavern. Paul mentioned he was producing a record by the Iveys at Apple Studios called "Come and Get It," the theme tune for the film Magic Christian. These were the same boys that had bedded down in our front room many times. Paul said he was thinking of changing their name to Finger.

"Ooh, that's bad," said Dad.

"Bad, Badfinger," Paul mused. "That's great, thanks Alf." And so Badfinger they became from that day on.

As we moved downstairs to the club, one of the groups Dad managed called the Curiosity Shoppe was rehearsing on stage. When they saw Paul they they were dumbstruck.

"Hi there." Paul waved at them.

We all followed Paul down the left-hand tunnel towards the band room. The original Cavern upright piano that the bailiffs had left behind still stood against the outside wall of the band room at the far end of the tunnel. Paul walked over to it and stood, because there was no piano stool, lifted the lid and started to play Hey Jude.

We were all transfixed. From the moment Paul began to sing, the whole experience seemed to unfold in slow motion. We were all in the moment together – pure magic. Hey Jude had been released in August and had its first public performance on the David Frost Show a few weeks later, but this was the only time Paul sang it at the Cavern. To this day I still get goose bumps every time I hear the song.

Paul with Curiosity Shoppe, Alf Geoghegan and Billy Butler (© Tracks Ltd.)

After loud appreciation from all of us he closed the piano lid, walked through the band-room and climbed the two steps on to the stage to join the Curiosity Shoppe in a number.

Sitting at the drums he confessed he'd always been a frustrated drummer. He was excited, like a child let loose in a sweet shop. Linda continued her photo shoot.

The photographs of Paul with me in the Top Bar and Paul with Dad, Paddy Delaney, Billy Butler and the Curiosity Shoppe on stage today hang in the Cavern to the right of the bar.

All too soon it was time for them to leave. Paul signed the visitors' book. "Second time around," he wrote, drawing a heart with an arrow through it. The visitors' book can be seen today at The Beatles Story at Liverpool's Albert Dock.

Paul said it had been a very special visit for him. He told us he'd always wanted to return to the Cavern, which held such a wealth of memories, and show Linda where it all began. Paul was the only Beatle to return to the Cavern while we owned it. The trouble with an historic moment is that you don't know how big it is until it is over.

He thanked Dad for a wonderful afternoon and for not informing the Press.

"My pleasure," Dad said. "We understand we had to be discreet and are thrilled that you wanted to come back to the Cavern." He gave Paul a red Cavern T-shirt as a souvenir. A photograph of Paul wearing it is displayed in the Cavern today.

As Paul and Linda were leaving, the lads from the Fruit Exchange opposite were unloading a wagon. One of them shouted in a broad Scouse accent, "Get yer 'err cut, McCaaartney."

Paul waved and smiled. "All right, lads," he shouted, as he got into his car with Linda and disappeared down Mathew Street.

Elated but anxious whether the photographs would turn out, Dad rang the photographer and explained he had some sensitive negatives to develop. He asked if he could he bring them and wait while they were processed. We took the camera to Jason's, a few hundred yards from the Cavern. Dad kept a tight grip on his brand new Yashica, which hopefully contained some wonderful memories.

In Jason's darkroom Dad handed over the camera and with bated breath we watched as Jason developed the roll of film. The negatives slowly turned into photographs and it soon became clear that each one was perfect. It was such a relief. We waited impatiently as Jason hung them up to dry and finally got them in a folder to take back to the Cavern office. We didn't realise that Linda was a professional photographer.

A few days later we received a postcard from Paul saying thanks again for everything. This postcard is also on view at The Beatles Story at the Albert Dock.

The following Saturday night at about 9 p.m. I was on the Cavern pay desk when the phone rang. An operator in America asked me if I would accept a collect call. Not knowing who it was, I refused because we'd had problems with groups phoning Australia and America at our expense – we'd had a pay phone installed to solve this problem.

The operator then asked me to hold and eventually connected the call.

"Who's that?" asked the caller.

"It's Deb," I replied. "Who's calling?"

"Oh, hi Deb, it's Paul, Paul McCartney. Is your Dad there?"

"Hi Paul, no, he's not here yet, he doesn't get in until about ten o'clock"

"I just wanted to say thanks for everything and any time your Dad feels like visiting Ohio, tell him to just let me know."

"OK Paul, I'll give him your message when he gets here, thanks for ringing."

I can only deduce that Paul had no change to make the call or was perhaps using someone else's phone – it sounded like he was in a restaurant or bar. Had I known it was him I would have readily accepted the charge. I had a queue of people waiting to come in as I chatted. I didn't make the obvious excuse, as they wouldn't have believed me anyway. Paddy Delaney was beside himself on hearing I had been talking to Paul McCartney while he'd been pacifying all the patrons waiting in line.

When Dad arrived he was very touched and sorry he'd missed his call. He never got the time to take Paul up on his offer.

In 1973, five years after Paul and Linda visited us at the Cavern, Paul returned to Liverpool to play at the Empire Theatre with his new band, Wings. In a dressing room interview he told a reporter from the *Liverpool Echo* (oddly enough, called George Harrison), "It's a funny feeling coming back to Liverpool after so long away from the scene. I wasn't even sure how the folk would take me, but they were marvellous tonight. Fantastic, and when they started jiving in the aisles and jumping on the seats, I just thought, this is where it all began."

He was right. At the old Cavern, when he and the other Beatles rocked and rolled, even the spiders ran for cover.

"The strange thing is," he added, "the stuff that really turns them on is the old rock and roll. They listen to the other numbers but it isn't until we hit the rock that we get them going. Funny really, it means that we are back where we started, for it was the hard beat rock we played and sang at the Cavern in our early days that used to get the fans away. Ten years later it still works."

On 4th December 1969, Dad received a letter from his friend Bill Collins, manager of the Iveys, now Badfinger.

> *Dear Alf:*
>
> *Herewith the latest Iveys Badfinger record, hope you like it! Listen to the 'B' side, it takes me back to the band-room at the Cavern, with The Beatles on stage pounding away. (Paul is on piano by the way).*

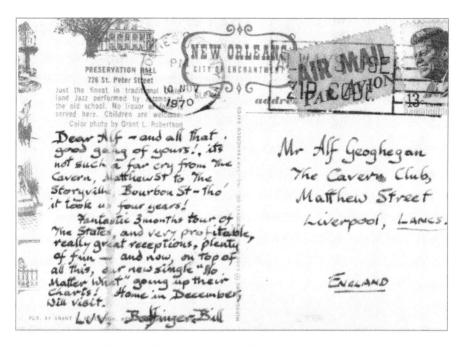

Postcard from Badfinger manager Bill Collins on the band's US tour

The 'A' side is the theme of Magic Christian, from the sound-track, written and produced by Paul and will get a lot of publicity, one way and another.

You know that Ron left some weeks ago and settled down to domesticity, well, we've now got a new man and from where? The Pool, of course. You probably know Joey Molland well, he's been working with Billy Kinsley lately.

Thanks for your past co-operation, Alf. I hope you play our record at the club and we get together again before long.

Yours with affection,

Bill Collins

The song was "Come and Get It," written and produced by Paul McCartney, which became a big hit in both the UK and the US. Tommy Evans, lead singer on the track, first played in a group called the Calderstones before the Iveys recruited him. He later said, "Paul was the local hero at home. We both lived on a prefab estate in Knowsley. But I never dreamed then that I'd end up working with him like this."

Badfinger had another top ten hit in 1970 with "No Matter What" and then Tommy and Pete Ham wrote "Without You." Harry Nilsson's version became one of the biggest hits of 1972, a chart-topper in at least five countries. Tommy and Pete won the British Academy's Ivor Novello Award for Best Song Musically and Lyrically.

Pete Ham tragically committed suicide in 1975 and the group broke up. In 1978 Tommy reformed Badfinger with Joey Molland but tragedy struck once more when in 1983 Tommy Evans also committed suicide.

Coincidentally, several weeks before Paul's visit, Dad had started to organise a music festival at The Mystery, a local park in Wavertree, in aid of the Save the Children Fund. Dad had already approached Eric Beard, a famous runner and personal friend.

Dad wrote to Paul asking for his support:

Dear Paul,

On the 22nd November at 2.30 p. m. Eric Beard, the well-known runner will start a marathon run around the perimeter of Wavertree Park and will keep going for twenty four hours.

He will be joined by Showbiz personalities and the Lord Mayor of Liverpool will fire the starting gun for the show to begin, to celebrate the Jubilee Year of the Save the Children Fund.

I have been asked to contribute and for my part will be organizing a Beat Festival in the park to take place whilst the Run is in progress.

I have approximately seven weeks to arrange the event and to decide who will attend and who will perform. Can I meet you to discuss the possibility of you and the rest of the boys attending and any local groups playing and you joining in with one or two of your numbers, or John and Yoko appearing?

This will be Liverpool's first Open Air Concert in the Park and being for such a good cause I think we could all help immensely, don't you? The Queen Mother is President of the Save the Children Fund and Mr. Rushworth and Mr. B. Smallman who is Professor of Music at Liverpool University are members of the Committee.

A proportion of the Fund each year subsidises 2000 children in Youth Makes Music and they perform each year at the Philharmonic Hall in Liverpool.

Also on Tuesday 18th November at 2 p.m. at the Cavern, a reception will be held to launch this Festival and Marathon Run.

Invitations will be going out to Television, Press, Civic heads and Showbiz people and do hope you will be in a position to attend this time having missed the re-opening of the Cavern in 1966 due to your commitments.

I look forward to a phone call if a meeting is possible when I could call on you to explain further "what's what" and "who's who" and any advice you can offer on this very special occasion.

Yours Sincerely

Alf Geoghegan

Invitations went out from the Cavern. Dad ended his appeal for support with the words: "Liverpool is calling on: Ken Dodd, Frankie Vaughan, Arthur Askey, Ted Ray, Jimmy Tarbuck, Kenny Everett, Cilla Black, Derrick Nimmo, Gerry Marsden, Norman Vaughan, Derick Guyler, Rita Tushingham, Arthur Dooley, Peter Maloney, Norman Rossington, Neville Smith, Peter Adamson, Les Dawson, Rupert Davies, John Gregson, Rex Harrison, Tommy Ward, Alun Owen, The Scaffold, The Spinners, The Beatles, The Liverpool Scene, The Searchers, The Tremeloes, Kenneth Cope, Etc. Etc."

Dad also sent an invitation to the Prime Minister, which Eric Beard had personally delivered to 10 Downing Street. Harold Wilson apologised that he could not attend due to a previous engagement in London.

THE DIRECTORS OF THE CAVERN, LIVERPOOL

request the pleasure of your company at a

RECEPTION

to celebrate the Golden Jubilee of the

SAVE THE CHILDREN FUND

on

TUESDAY, 18TH NOVEMBER, 1969, AT 2 P.M.

R.S.V.P.
To the Secretary
The Cavern
8-12 Mathew Street
Liverpool
Tel. 051-236 7881

Guests are kindly requested to endeavour to attend by 1-30 p.m.

Then two days before the reception we received the devastating news that Eric Beard had been killed in a road accident. The music festival was cancelled but the reception at the Cavern went ahead as planned.

After helping prepare food for the reception, I had to dash home to change into a silver crocheted strappy mini dress bought for the occasion. I had roughly an hour and a half to shower, dress and rush back to the club before celebrities and guests started to arrive.

The Cavern was full of celebrities and showbiz people. Press and TV crews were milling around, local groups provided entertainment and waiters were constantly replenishing empty glasses. The two-day event was a great success and raised a lot of money for The Save the Children Fund. But it was cloaked in sadness over the premature death of our dear friend Eric Beard in such tragic circumstances.

A Bent Copper and his Mates

The first moment I had an inkling of something sinister taking place in our lives was when Dad said to me one day, "You'll be getting a phone call tonight at the club and I want you to remember every word you say and every word the caller says, because you may be asked to repeat it at a later date."

I was very concerned but didn't question him. I knew he would tell me what it was all about when he was ready. The call he was expecting came through that evening while I was on the pay desk. I wrote down, word for word, a transcript of my brief conversation with the caller and gave it to Dad when I got home.

I still didn't know what was going on but knew it had to be something serious. The conversation went something like this:

"Good evening, the Cavern Club."

A man's voice: "Could I speak to Mr Geoghegan."

"I'm sorry he's not here, can I help?"

"No, it's OK, I'll ring him at home."

"Can I ask who's calling?" The caller gave his name. "I'll tell him you called."

A few days later Dad told me what was happening. A young plain-clothes constable from A Division in Liverpool City Police, who had been a member of the vice squad for eleven weeks, had approached Dad at the club around 10 p.m. on 30th April 1969.

He asked if there was anywhere where they could talk privately, so Dad took him through to the office, where the policeman asked him: "Have the London boys called on you yet because they are in Liverpool on takeover bids?"

Being a man of the world and an astute businessman, Dad weighed up three possible scenarios. Firstly, the copper could be referring to legitimate London club owners looking to extend their empires by purchasing an interest in a Liverpool club. Secondly, London heavies could be thinking about setting up a protection racket. Thirdly, someone had plans to use the Cavern as a distribution point for drugs, a trend in many London clubs.

Dad wasn't stupid. He answered that the London boys hadn't been to see him and furthermore he wasn't interested in bids for the Cavern.

The constable then told him that the Cavern had been discussed by his Inspector and was to be raided soon but no date had been set.

"Is anybody looking after you, Mr Geoghegan?" asked the officer.

"I don't know what you mean," Dad replied.

"Is anybody in the police looking after you?" he repeated.

Dad played stupid. "We have a wonderful relationship with the police and if ever we need them they act very quickly. I've no complaints at all about the way they look after us here."

"No, you don't understand, Mr Geoghegan. Is anybody looking after you?"

Dad knew all along where this was leading but he waited for him to spell it out. The policeman then explained he could tip him off with the date of any proposed police raid of the club.

"Oh, I see," he said, as if the penny had just dropped. "What did you have in mind?"

"Well I think a fiver a week would do to start," replied the policeman.

Thinking on his feet, Dad decided to stall so he could assess this situation. "Oh, OK, call in and see me next week."

"I was thinking we could start now, Mr Geoghegan, and then I could come and see you each week."

"That's a bit difficult, as I don't have anything on me tonight. Give me a ring tomorrow night and I'll arrange a time with you." Dad gave him the phone number.

Dad couldn't abide this sort of behaviour. The following day, 1st May 1969, he reported his encounter with the police officer to the Chief Constable.

The police acted very swiftly. Two senior police officers, Detective Chief Superintendent Davies and Detective Inspector Wynne, asked Dad to arrange to meet the policeman at noon the following Friday. They arrived at our house in the morning and rigged up a recorder in our living room with a microphone hidden in a two-bar electric fire they'd placed in the front room hearth.

They asked Dad to take everything out of his pockets and gave him a marked five-pound note to give to the policeman. I had never seen Dad so nervous. He said he felt sick to his boots. The officers told him what to say and to keep it short and not make conversation. Mum and I were in the back room listening in with the senior officers.

The knock finally came at the door. As he showed the policeman into the front room, he tried to engage Dad in small talk.

"I'm sorry," Dad interrupted, addressing the policeman by his first name. "I've got rather a busy day. A fiver, wasn't it?" That was the pre-arranged cue that the deed was done.

"Yes, that's right." The policeman took the marked five-pound note, put it in his pocket and shook Dad's hand.

As Dad opened the front-room door to show the policeman out, the two officers were waiting for him in the hall. They asked him to produce the five-pound note that Mr. Geoghegan had given him. "What five-pound note?" he replied.

When told he would be searched, he produced the money and lied that the five pounds was for a debt. The senior officers arrested him on the spot and took him away.

Dad was in a terrible state. Shaking, he rushed to the bathroom to be physically sick. He cried all afternoon, saying he felt awful after what had happened and especially after shaking the copper's hand.

The police officer was subsequently charged with attempting to extort money from my father.

It affected us all deeply, but this was only the beginning. Leading up to the trial we were subjected to constant harassment. Police would descend on the bands playing at the club, saying they were looking for drugs.

One night we were raided by a large contingent of police, including several WPCs. One regular visitor was furious and made her way to the front desk and burst out, "What's going on, Mr. Geoghegan? There are policewomen all over the girls in the toilets looking for drugs. We've told them if they're looking for drugs, they're in the wrong club and we told them to f*** off."

None of the raids turned up any drugs.

Shortly before the trial I overheard and documented a brief conversation at the Cavern entrance between Paddy Delaney and a policeman. It went as follows:

Policeman: "Aren't you afraid of being knocked off?"

Paddy Delaney: "What do you mean?"

Policeman: "Every other club has."

On Wednesday 30th July 1969 the policeman appeared on committal proceedings at Liverpool City Magistrates Court. After hearing the charges and the evidence against him, the justices committed the policeman for trial at Liverpool Crown Court on a corruption charge.

Before the trial another incident took place in Greenbank Road, where we lived. The Cavern Club manager, Norman Clarke, who didn't have a car, would accompany me home in my Mini after we closed, as I usually carried the night's takings. He would then drive himself home in my car and pick me up the following day.

After waving goodbye I went into the house and straight upstairs. From my bedroom I heard a deafening noise of screeching brakes and dashed to the window to see what was happening.

With a clear view I saw at least five cars surrounding my Mini. Norman was out of the car and leaning against it. He had only gone a few hundred yards when they descended on him and forced him to a stop.

As soon as I realised what was happening, I was out of the house in a flash, running to the scene. The five unmarked cars contained plain-clothes police officers, who were desperately trying to get Norman to open the boot of my car.

I knew this was not normal police procedure – converging out of nowhere on a car that had only gone a few hundred yards. I believe they call this sort of thing a hard strike.

"What's going on?" I shouted as I ran towards them.

"Is this your car?"

"Yes, what's the problem?" I was on high alert after all we had suffered in the past months.

"Does this person have permission to drive it?"

"Yes, he does."

"We need to see in the boot." They were threatening.

As soon as they said that, I wasn't going to take any chances. Every incident so far had been staged to somehow link the club or us with drugs. They weren't getting the opportunity to plant drugs in my car.

Norman was leaning against the car with his arms firmly folded.

"There is nothing in the boot and I've decided that I'm taking the car back home. Give me the keys." Norman handed me the keys.

"We need to see in the boot," one of them said.

"There's nothing in the boot and I'm taking the car back home."

"We need to check it," he insisted.

"I've told you there's nothing in it." I was angry but determined not to lose my cool. I told Norman to run back to our house and tell Dad to phone the police while I waited.

"There's no need for that, we are the police." His tone was less angry. Norman ran back to the house.

"On this occasion, we'll let you go," one of them said, gesturing to the others to back off.

I got into my car and drove it the short distance home. By this time everyone in the house was awake and wondering what the commotion was about. It was obvious that the police at the station had no knowledge of this hard strike.

Dad delayed ringing the police until the following day so he could contact the two senior officers handling the case on their direct line. It was also three o'clock in the morning.

We documented everything that had happened. Norman told us they came out of every side road all at once, braking hard and forcing him to stop. One of the five men ordered him out of the car and tried to bully him into opening the boot.

God knows how many incidents Dad had to report to the officer in charge of the case. We were on high alert every day leading up to the trial. They were trying to wear us down, especially Dad, the main witness. I was incensed when one night he told me he was almost ready to give up and drop the case.

"He's somebody's son, what about his poor parents?"

He was too bloody sympathetic for my liking and I was furious.

"Don't you dare! Are you mad? That shower of bastards will turn the tables on you and, if they have their way, it will be you in a prison cell, not the bent copper. Do you think he'll care that you're somebody's Dad or husband? After all you've been through for the last seven months, you know this guy has a lot of friends trying their damnedest to pin drugs on you."

The Liverpool Echo, Friday, November 7, 1969 13

City P.C. gaoled 15 months

Liverpool police constable Thomas Alan Green, aged 22, of 145 Queens Drive, Liverpool 13, was gaoled for 15 months by Mr. Justice Brabin at Liverpool Crown Court, yesterday, for corruption.

The judge told him: "When a police officer is found guilty on the sort of evidence that has been called in this case it must be underlined that this is a serious matter. If a policeman is corrupt, how can people live safely under the law?

"There is no suggestion that you were seduced from your duty by someone else," added the judge. "You went searching for that which constitutes corruption."

He said he took into account in sentencing Green that those with whom he would serve his imprisonment would not take kindly to having a former policeman in their company.

"Therefore prison will be harder for you than for other persons. Nevertheless, it is essential on the evidence produced in this case, that you serve a sentence of imprisonment."

Microphone

Cavern Club proprietor Mr Alfred Henry Geoghegan told the court that Green, for eleven weeks a member of the vice squad, had called at his club and offered to tip him off about police raids for £5 a week. He reported this to police headquarters.

A week later two senior police officers in the next room at Mr Geoghegan's home listened over a microphone to a conversation in which Green, who had called there by appointment, accepted a £5 note from the Cavern Club proprietor. They then arrested him.

Green, pleading not guilty, said he had been trying to buy drugs from Mr Geoghegan in the course of his duty. The five pounds mentioned in the conversation his senior officers overheard related to 5lb. weight of cannabis he was attempting to buy. He alleged that the £5 note found in his pocket had been planted there by Mr Geoghegan.

"She's right, Alf." Mum was upset. "You mustn't give up."

On Monday 3rd November 1969, the trial took place at Liverpool Crown Court. In the witness stand I was asked to repeat the conversation between myself and the policeman that my Dad had so solemnly asked me to remember many months before.

We were right to be very alert leading up to the trial, as the defence suggested that Dad was trying to sell drugs to the officer. The accused was trying to imply that Dad had a storeroom full of drugs at the club and the mention of five pounds related to the weight of drugs he was being offered.

The prosecution retorted, "Have you any idea what five pounds of drugs looks like? Are you suggesting that Mr Geoghegan had rows and rows of bags of drugs on shelves, like bags of sugar?"

On Thursday November 6th 1969, the accused was found guilty of corruption and sentenced to fifteen months in prison by Mr. Justice Brabin.

Sentencing him, the judge told him, "When a police officer is found guilty on the sort of evidence that has been called in this case, it must be underlined that this is a serious matter. If a policeman is corrupt, how can people live safely under the law? There is no suggestion that you were seduced from your duty by someone else. You went searching for that which constitutes corruption."

The Judge said that he took into account in sentencing him that those with whom he would serve his imprisonment would not take kindly to having a former policeman in their company.

"Therefore, prison will be harder for you than for other persons. Nevertheless, it is essential on the evidence produced in this case that you serve a sentence of imprisonment.

When Christmas arrived some weeks later, we received a card from the policeman's parents saying, "I hope you will have as Happy a Christmas as we will have." Mum and Dad were extremely stressed out about everything that had taken place and didn't need the bitterness of his parents.

If this policeman had not coming looking for easy pickings from a protection racket, none of it would have happened. He just didn't bank on anyone doing the right thing and standing up to him. Dad was the kindest and the most caring and upright person in the world but he was nobody's fool. It took us years to recover from our ordeal and even as I write this I feel the pangs of hurt my Mum and Dad had to endure.

GOOD TIMES AGAIN

We continued to bring big names to the Cavern. On Friday 18th October 1968 Gary Walker from The Walker Brothers appeared with his band the Rain. Friday 11th April 1969, the Zombies were on stage. Monday 28th July, the Scaffold appeared, backed by Business.

The *Liverpool Echo* carried a story that in August 1969 a young Bill Clinton, who was studying at Oxford University, reportedly made a rare visit to the Grapes Pub in Mathew Street.

An unruly German nationalist berated Ringo Starr, who was in the pub at the time, shouting, "You've screwed up the world." He then pulled out a metal bar from his clothing to attack Ringo.

Also in the pub on the day was Cavern doorman Paddy Delaney, who later recalled that a young American he claims was Bill Clinton leapt forward and grabbed the German by the neck and overpowered him. Paddy held the culprit until the police arrived. We can only assume that the future US President's purpose in visiting Mathew Street was to visit the Cavern.

We now had a drinks licence and also served food in the Top Bar, a very successful move that enabled us to extend our licencing hours. But still we needed more space. Always ready for another project, Dad decided to look at No. 12 sitting empty beyond the club walls.

We broke through from the Cavern into this large, dank and dusty space, which was practically a carbon copy of the club running parallel to the Cavern's left tunnel. Huge iron rings were attached to the walls were probably "slave rings." Provision merchants who occupied the warehouses more than a century before probably brought in slaves with their general cargo of sugar cane and bananas. Not something Liverpool can be proud of. It made my skin crawl to see them.

This time we brought in subcontractors to build a large square bar in the centre of the space with easy access from the club. And so the Mersey Bar was born.

The Mersey Bar

The Cavern was now at its peak again and even with all the extra space was full most nights. We also built a kitchen and a large restaurant which ran the whole length of the Mersey Bar. The restaurant, open until the early hours, proved very popular with a varied menu of steak, curries, scampi and chicken dishes.

Now with our own restaurant on the premises, we no longer ended up around 3 a.m. at Alan Williams' Jacaranda in Slater Street for one of his great curries. Most of the groups would end up there after their gigs.

Not content with working all the hours that God sent, Dad decided to produce a weekly Cavern newspaper – and he expected me to help him. He was a workaholic and expected everybody else to be the same.

We printed on an enormous Xerox duplicator he bought, which a crew had managed to lift up the stairs into the then-unused boutique. There we were, printing and folding until the early hours every Sunday. *Cavern News* was free and very popular with members and visitors.

Nowadays the Cavern is well and truly established as one of the country's great tourist attractions for people of all ages from every part

of the planet. The trend was in place by late 1969, as this extract from
Cavern News suggests:

Overseas Visitors

*The holidays are in full swing and the popularity of the Cavern
is as great if not greater than ever it was where visitors from
overseas are concerned. At this time of the year the Cavern has
droves of sightseers wanting to see what, by now, must be "the
most wanted place to see on this earth." From the greatest cities
to the heart of the jungles of South Africa they call in to see the
Cavern and this includes civic dignitaries whose main wish for
visiting England is to see the birthplace of The Beatles and to
hear the most popular music of today's generation.*

There was a nasty accident in the Top Bar one night when a girl
slipped and fell on a broken glass and severely cut her leg. An ambu-
lance rushed her to hospital for emergency treatment with no serious
consequences. But from that day on Dad decided to supply drinks only
in plastic cups as a safety precaution. It did not go down well with the
customers and it took a lot of talk by staff and management to convince
patrons it was in everybody's best interests.

Among the big names now being booked at the club was Status Quo,
who arrived on Monday 9th February 1970 with enormous Vox speakers which they stacked at either side of the stage – plus a second row
stacked next to them just as high. This left barely enough room for the
band to fit in the middle, as the Cavern stage was really quite small, but
somehow they managed it.

It turned out to be a fabulous night with Status Quo full of energy
that electrified the atmosphere. The sound was mind-blowing, the whole
joint was jumping – and so were the speakers. At one point one of the
speakers wobbled dangerously but one of the group nudged it back into
position and carried on singing.

Nobody had heard of Queen when they played the Cavern on Saturday
31st October 1970. Ken Testi said, "I was the social secretary at St Helen's
College and I saw Freddie Mercury when he got in with a local band, Ibex,
at the Bolton Octagon. Then Freddie formed Queen with Brian May and
Roger Taylor and I wanted to put them on at the college but we needed
somewhere else to make the trip pay. Alf Geoghegan very kindly gave us a
gig at the Cavern as he had booked Ibex in the past."

Something for Everyone ! !

- **BONZO DOG DOO DAH BAND**
- **ESCORTS**
- **SCAFFOLD**
- **WILD WILD KLUBS**
- **MERSEYSIPPI JAZZ BAND**
- **BRIAN PATTEN**
- **TAMLA DISC SHOW**

Through the Looking Glass Fashion Parade

Comperes: Bob Wooler - Billy Butler - Ronnie Pimlett

all night happening
TWELVE - HOUR - NON - STOP - RAVE - UP

SATURDAY 10TH. JUNE 1967
7 p.m. Saturday - 7 a.m. Sunday

Snacks . Sandwiches . Late Licensed Bar (App: for)

CAVERN CLUB
MATHEW STREET (OFF NORTH JOHN STREET) LIVERPOOL

Tickets 12/6

FROM: NORTH EAST LIVERPOOL TECHNICAL COLLEGE (Phone STA 1388)
RUSHWORTH'S (ROY 8070 & Birkenhead 647 - 7723) , CAVERN CLUB (CEN 7881/3959

A NORTH EAST LIVERPOOL TECHNICAL COLLEGE PRESENTATION IN
AID OF THEIR, JULY SAHARA EXPEDITION

Hear all about this Fantastic Show on
RADIO CAROLINE

Hurry for your Tickets now

Freddie Mercury was living in rented accommodation in Penny Lane when he joined Ibex. He left them in late 1969 to join Brian May and Roger Taylor after an impromptu performance with them in a small Liverpool venue called The Sink, a cellar club in Hardman Street under a café called The Rumble n Tum.

It didn't make economic sense for them to travel all the way from London for what the college could pay them, so Dad agreed to let them double up at the Cavern as a favour. The gig was pretty much a selection of the material that went on the first Queen album. It was obvious the group had star potential. As was often the case, being stuck at the pay desk I missed their performance, but by all accounts they brought the house down.

Dad was irritated that the Cavern's drinks licence had to be renewed every year, so would take his licencing law book to bed to figure out a way to overcome this inconvenience. He often fell asleep sitting up in bed, still clutching the book. Mum called it his bible. Some nights he hardly slept.

"There must be a way to extend this period, there must be a way," was his refrain. After months of tireless searching his eureka moment arrived.

"Got it! I've found a loophole." He was so excited he couldn't wait to get to the solicitor's office the next day. When he suggested to Leslie Black, of Black Davidson & Co., that he wanted him to apply for a ten-year licence for the Cavern, the solicitor thought Dad was barking mad.

"You'll never get it, it's never been heard of." He tried to dissuade him.

"Look, Leslie," Dad said, "You can't deny that there is a loophole here and I'm instructing you to apply for a ten-year licence."

"OK, Alf, but I don't think you have a chance of getting it."

After several meetings between the solicitor and the licencing committee, he got it! It was the only ten-year licence ever granted in Liverpool as the local licensing regulations were changed soon after that to ensure that it never happened again

One Saturday every month we would hold a daytime event at the club for various charities. My mother would beg gifts and contributions from all the local businesses.

Kingsize Taylor & The Dominoes

The Fruit Exchange opposite the club was very generous and always gave us crates of fruit. One day my mother caught Harry Isaacson, a director of a local beer bottling plant and a very wealthy man, taking an apple out of one of the crates in the Cavern. He was about to take a bite when she came up behind him and shouted, stopping him in his tracks.

Harry Isaacson, you ought to be ashamed of yourself, stealing from little children."

"For God's sake woman, it's only an apple," he snapped.

"Yes but it's not your apple. Either give me a donation or put it back."

She shamed him into making a decision. He did put the apple back but didn't give a donation.

We held a lot of charity events, raising money for Save the Children, the Royal School for the Blind, the Spastic Society, Merseyside Children's Homes and Orphanages, Cancer Research Foundation and many others.

Dad hosted a Christmas party for over two hundred homeless and orphaned children at the Cavern on 23rd December 1966, making sure they all received a Christmas present. I have dozens of letters of thanks from the children and from the proprietors of the homes. Local businesses contributed with food, gifts, party hats and balloons. It was a memorable occasion for Mum and Dad. At the time I was still up to my eyes in turkeys, geese and legs of pork frantically getting Christmas orders together in the butcher's shops.

We also held events for the School for the Deaf. The first time we held one such event I remember Dad being enthralled as he watched everybody picking up on the vibrations and dancing in time to the rhythm of the music. He said it was one of the most amazing things he'd ever seen.

5th October,

COLIN MYLER PRESENTS THE FIRST NEW TEENSCENES

THE
CAVERN

No. 10 Mathew Street, Liverpool, is where it all began. In the small, dimly-lit and crowded cellar the Lennon and McCartney partnership was launched. And just four years after it opened the Cavern became a legend in its own lifetime.

Today, eight years later, one wonders has some of the Cavern's image been rubbed off? One thing is certainly evident. It is no longer a place for just the swingin' teenager. In the past three years it has been extended, redesigned—except for the Cavern itself that is—and attractively furnished.

Now you can sit down to a steak, relax in plush carpeted lounges, or dance in its discotheque.

The man who has given the club this sophisticated look is its owner, 60-years-old Mr. Alf Geoghegan. Two years ago, a year after he had bought the club for £5,500, Mr. Geoghegan sold his four Liverpool butchers shops and concentrated on reshaping the club.

It has cost him 'a lot of money,' but he doesn't think of his cheque book, only of the end-product. He is a shrewd business man, likes writing songs and has no ambitions to become a millionaire or own a yacht. He just wants to do what's right.

Next to his family, the club is his whole life. 'There is no doubt that the Cavern is a shrine,' he said assuredly. 'People living in and around Liverpool do not appreciate how well-known it is simply because they are living on its doorstep. But every year almost 6,000 international visitors come to the Cavern, and we have around 2,300 members.

'And how much is the club worth now,' I asked him. 'That's easily answered,' he replied. 'The value of the Cavern is the price Liverpool wants to put on it. I would not sell it for anything. For the first time in my life I am doing something I really enjoy . . . you can't buy happiness, can you?'

Mr. Alfred Geoghegan outside the club which, after his family has become 'his whole life.' On the other side of this unpretentious door, in one of Liverpool's old streets, is perhaps the world's most famous beat-club—'The Cavern.'

Alf outside the Cavern
(courtesy Liverpool Echo/Trinity Mirror)

THE WRECKING CREW

The Club was at its peak in late September 1970 when Dad was approached by Harry Waterman with an offer to buy the Cavern. This came out of the blue as my Dad had never considered selling the club.

"Leave it with me," he said, needing time to think about it.

But why on earth would he sell the Cavern? It was more successful now than it had ever been. On the other hand, the best time to sell a business is at its peak.

Dad had meanwhile expanded his business interests with a taxi garage from where he ran and maintained a small fleet of Hackney cabs. He'd put a lot of his time in at the garage for the past couple of years, a trade he knew inside out.

Now that I was running the Cavern, he only occasionally popped into the club on evenings and weekends. We'd also taken on a manager the year before to oversee the logistics of the entertainment side of the business. Dad sat on Harry's offer for a while.

Harry Waterman and Harry Isaacson (the guy who took the apple) owned Kings Bottling Works in Garston and a lot of clubs in Liverpool, including the Wooky Hollow, the Coconut Grove, the Pyramid, the Temple, Pez Espada, Annabelle's, Wispa, Allinsons and Hickory Lodge. But none of them could hold a candle to the Cavern.

Their modus operandi was to supply beer and spirits on favourable credit terms to small independent club owners and not press them too hard for payment for maybe six months. Then they would go in heavy with legal demands for immediate payment, which in most cases could not be met. They could then buy the assets of the club for a song and take them over.

At one time they were rumoured to control more than a dozen Liverpool licenced premises. They were nicknamed Wagon and Trailer because Waterman would always go in first followed by Isaacson (also

No.............................   [LIVERPOOL AND BIRKENHEAD]

IN PARLIAMENT.
    SESSION 1970–71.

BRITISH RAILWAYS BOARD

Tel.: 051-227 3911   c/o TOWN CLERK, LIVERPOOL,
Ext. 378   P.O. BOX No. 88,
                                               MUNICIPAL BUILDINGS,
                                                    DALE STREET,
                                               LIVERPOOL L69 2DH.

                                                  17th November, 1970.

SIR(S) or MADAM,

                        BRITISH RAILWAYS (No. 2) BILL

       I beg to inform you that application is intended to be made to Parliament in the present Session
for leave to introduce this Bill.

       I understand that your interest in the property mentioned in the annexed Schedule is as stated
therein. If the Bill passes into law, the property mentioned in the said Schedule, or a right to use the same,
will be liable to be acquired compulsorily under the powers of the Act.

       Plans and Sections with a Book of Reference thereto relating to the works proposed to be carried
out and the lands proposed to be acquired or used under the powers sought in the Bill will be, on or before
the 20th November, 1970, deposited for public inspection as follows (that is to say) : as regards the works
and lands in the city of Liverpool, with the Town Clerk of Liverpool at his office at Municipal Buildings,
Liverpool (Room 201, Top Floor), and as regards the works and lands in the county borough of Birkenhead,
with the Town Clerk of Birkenhead at his office at the Town Hall, Birkenhead. On the said Plans your
property is designated by the number or numbers in the annexed Schedule.

       If the annexed Schedule contains any error or misdescription will you kindly inform me at the above
address at your earliest convenience ?

       Copies of the Bill will be, on or before the 4th December next, deposited for public inspection and
for sale at my offices and the offices of the Board's Parliamentary Agents at the addresses set out on the
back of this notice ; and also at the office of the Town Clerk, Municipal Buildings, Liverpool (Room 201,
Top Floor), and the office of the Town Clerk, Town Hall, Birkenhead.

       Objection to the Bill may be made by depositing a Petition against it. I shall be pleased, on
receiving from you a request in writing, to inform you in due course of the latest date on which you may
deposit a Petition in either House. For your present information, the latest date for depositing a Petition
against the Bill in the first House is the 6th February, if the first House is the House of Lords, or the
30th January, if the first House is the House of Commons. The latest date for depositing a Petition against
the Bill in the second House is the tenth day after that on which the Bill receives its first reading in that
House. If this date is a Sunday, Christmas Day or a Bank Holiday, or a day on which the House does not
sit, the final date for depositing may be postponed.

       Copies of the Standing Orders of both Houses of Parliament relating to the time and mode of
presenting Petitions in opposition to Bills are annexed hereto.

       I further beg to inform you that it is intended that the Act shall authorise the compulsory acquisition
of the subsoil or undersurface of the land comprising or forming part of the property mentioned in the
annexed Schedule, or of easements or rights in such property, in any case where only such subsoil or
undersurface, or only such easements or rights, are required.

                        I am, Sir(s) or Madam,

                        Your most obedient Servant,

                                          EVAN HARDING,
                                                 Solicitor.

To   Alfred Geoghegan,

          52 Greenbank Road,

              Liverpool, 18.

known as Harry Ike). They tried their usual tactic with Dad but he made sure to settle their account in full each month. He was no mug. The Cavern was one club they weren't going to pick up for a song.

Harry had a front man called Roy Adams who had always dreamed of owning the Cavern, having spent most of his working life on the doors of Liverpool clubs.

In October 1970 Harry Waterman approached Dad again with a firm offer to buy the Cavern. With the Club at its peak and Dad heavily involved in his taxi business, it seemed like a good time to sell.

Once the purchase price had been agreed upon, contracts were drawn up and signed. Harry Waterman insisted that I stay on until the end of January 1971 to get Harry's partner, Roy Adams, up to speed on the day-to-day running of the club.

A few weeks after signing the contract Dad received a Notice of Intent from solicitors acting on behalf of British Rail, which owned the land on which the Cavern stood. The legal document advised that they intended to present a bill before the next session of Parliament which, if passed, would give British Rail the power to compulsorily purchase the site of the Cavern in connection with their plans to construct the new underground railway network in Liverpool and their intention was to build one of the ventilation shafts in Mathew Street on the site of the Cavern.

However, they said that if the owners of the Cavern paid £500 to British Rail, they were prepared to re-site it further down Mathew Street nearer to Button Street.

I can remember on at least three occasions before the sale was finalised witnessing Dad telephoning Harry Waterman and telling him about the letter he had received. The conversations were always the same, each time with more urgency.

"Harry, you must pay this money to British Rail," pleaded Dad. "The Cavern is a shrine to the world and every day streams of tourists arrive to see it. You mustn't lose it, you owe it to Liverpool and the world to save it. You can save it if you pay them the £500."

The proposed payment was a drop in the ocean to Harry Waterman.

"Well, Alfie, I'll let Roy decide," was his apathetic reply.

"You must tell him how important it is to save it," Dad insisted.

Dad rang his solicitor and told him about the Notice of Intent and begged him to persuade Harry to pay the money to British Rail. Dad

LESTER DAVIDSON
S. LESLIE BLACK
STEPHEN RALPH
BARRY H. DAVIDSON

BLACK, DAVIDSON & CO.

SOLICITORS

Alfred Geoghegan Esq,
52 Greenbank Road,
LIVERPOOL 18.

50B THE TEMPLE
24 DALE STREET, LIVERPOOL, L2 5RY

Telephone 051-236 5863 (7 lines)
Telegrams " Lex, Liverpool "

Our Ref: SLB/MVH/W.571.   Please ask for: Mr.Black.

Your Ref.

Date   24th November 1970.

Dear Mr.Geoghegan,

Re: The Cavern.

I have now prepared the necessary documents, and I have asked Mr.
Waterman and Mr. Adams to make an appointment to see me, it might
be as well, if you could call to see me at the same time, so that
any outstanding matter relating to the transaction can be discussed
and we can then save time. There is one matter that I would like
to mention, and that relates to any pending agreements which you may
have entered into in connection with the Club. Perhaps you will
kindly let me have a note of same, and if they are in writing, bring
the documents with you, Because this of course would be very
important. I would also like you to let me have the last receipt in
respect of the rent of the premises, and also relating to the rates
so that these matters can be attended to on completion.

What is the position with regard to the agreement with The Performing
Rights Society, and are there any other agreements relating to the
hire of equipment, and if so, what are they. "hat is also the position
with regard to all the chattels in the Club, has Mr. Adams and yourself
agreed an inventory, because this is absolutely necessary to annexe to
the agreement, and if this has not been done the quicker that you can
get together and do it the better, otherwise this will hold up the
arrangements. I would also like you to let me have the Registration
Certificate, that is the 10 year Certificate, and the other extensions
which we have from time to time obtained, so that these can be shown to
the Purchasers, and I think that you should also bring with you the
Members' Book and a copy of the Rules so that they may be fully aware of
the contents thereof. In other words,I think they should be put in
possession of all the relevant and pertinent matters appertaining to the
Club so that they cannot say, that they did not see anything or were not
told anything. This is absolutely important and consequently if I have
omitted to raise any point about anything which goes on in the Club or
which you have done on the premises, then please raise it at the
Meeting so that it can be discussed and disposed of. Sorry to have
to write to you at such length, but I am sure you will appreciate
that this is the only way of satisfactorily having an expeditious
completion to the transaction.

Yours sincerely,

even gave his solicitor the original letter from British Rail for safekeeping. If only we'd made a photocopy of that letter.

Nobody thought of things like that in those days. Our thinking was that the solicitor had the letter, so it would be safely filed away.

In 2013 I contacted my Dad's solicitor at the time, Leslie Black, who was still practising law in his mid-90s. I told him who I was and asked him if he had in his archives any documents relating to my Dad and the sale of the Cavern and if it would be possible to access them.

I was taken aback by his hostility.

"That was forty years ago. No! There wouldn't be anything left," he snapped.

"Surely you would have some documents in your archives?" I tried again.

"We don't keep documents that long, I can't help you."

Even if he didn't have any documents, his reaction was inexplicably defensive. He was very cutting and I couldn't help thinking, "I wonder what he's trying to hide?"

I now know from the documentation I currently have that Leslie Black was acting for Harry Waterman and Roy Adams when they purchased the Cavern, while at the same time representing my Dad who was selling it. Surely that was a conflict of interest.

Harry Waterman had no attachment to the Cavern. It was just another club to him, another outlet that would make him more money. Making money was all Harry thought about, as one of Dad's stories indicates.

Walking down London Road in Liverpool with Dad one day, dressed in his signature scruffy old raincoat and trilby hat, a cigar dangling from his mouth, Harry bent down and picked up an empty beer bottle from the gutter and put it in his raincoat pocket. This was long before he'd expressed an interest in buying the Cavern.

"Harry, what are you doing?" Dad was shocked.

"A penny on that, Alfie," was his reply without missing a step, as if it was the normal thing to do. He said he'd put it in a crate back at Kings Bottling Company in Garston.

Another tale Dad told concerned Harry's stay at Lourdes Hospital for a minor operation. The hospital was on Greenbank Road, where we lived, so Dad would call in to see him every afternoon. Sister Marie

Flynn would wait for his arrival to ask for help with a problem over the phone, which was on a wheeled trolly.

"Mr. Geoghegan," she pleaded in her soft Irish drawl. "Would you please ask Mr. Waterman to give us the phone so that the other patients can use it? I've tried to take it but he refuses to stop using it,"

All day long Harry was wheeling and dealing while in hospital. Dad even drew him a cartoon of a hearse with a huge safe strapped to the top of it. The caption read: "Who says you can't take it with you?"

Stories aside, both Harry Waterman and Roy Adams knew about British Rail's intention to purchase the land during their negotiations to buy the Cavern – and long before the contracts were signed. They had the power to do something about it and pay the £500 to save the club's original premises. But for reasons best known to themselves, they chose not to.

I stayed on at the club for a hand-over period of a couple of months and left in January 1971. It was a very emotional day and I felt empty and bereaved leaving the Cavern for the last time.

I still have the original Notice of Intent from British Rail along with letters to the solicitor. The Cavern could have been saved and if Dad had still owned it there's no doubt the original Cavern would still be standing.

Dad was mortified at their decision to do nothing and was angry and distraught when the bulldozers moved in to demolish the Cavern in June 1973.

I remember him saying to me, "Knowing the phenomenon that is the Beatles and knowing how much the Cavern means to so many people, who in their right mind would allow it to be demolished? They had plenty of warning, why didn't they save it?"

DJ Bob Wooler sadly commented, "Strange, I thought, that no-one invited me to the last farewell."

As it happened British Rail didn't put the ventilation shaft in Mathew Street after all, so the Cavern was demolished for nothing.

It begs the question. Why did Roy Adams accept the Compulsory Purchase Order that was issued in late 1972 when he still had the chance of paying the £500 for British Rail to relocate the site of the proposed ventilation shaft? If British Rail didn't need the site after all and there was a chance that the Cavern could have been saved, why didn't he save it?

He'd had nearly three years to think about it. The Cavern was obviously just another club to him, otherwise he wouldn't have had to think twice about making the right decision. It wasn't just the Cavern Club and the cellar full of noise that was buried beneath the rubble, but a musical heritage that by right belonged to the world.

If Roy Adams was not prepared to save the Cavern, why did Liverpool Corporation not step in to save it? But then again, they had a track record of making bad decisions about iconic Liverpool structures. They allowed the Dockland Overhead Railway (known locally as the Dockers' Umbrella) to be demolished, didn't they?

Roy Adams opened a club across Mathew Street from the original Cavern in the then-vacant Fruit Exchange. The Cavern sign that my dad had designed was placed above the door.

Maybe the money he received from British Rail for the Compulsory Purchase Order for the Cavern was too tempting. Paying the £500 to have the site of the proposed ventilation shaft moved to save the Cavern would have meant no demolition.

Here lies the million dollar question. Was it worth paying £500 to British Rail and paying even more money for a new lease to save the world-famous Cavern Club? We'll never know.

Renegotiating the lease may have been the sticking point. The original lease Alan Sytner had signed in January 1957, when he opened the Cavern, was due to expire. The terms he negotiated were for a vacant and derelict building for which the landlords would have been thrilled to accept a low rent. The club's worldwide fame would mean a considerable increase in lease costs, with its value as a custom-built music venue also boosted by the extensive renovations carried out since 1957.

But surely, no amount of money was too much to save the most famous club in the world. Over the years I've been incensed to hear and read that the blame for the demolition of the Cavern Club was being firmly placed at my Dad's feet. It's time to set the record straight.

My Dad was a prolific songwriter and was interviewed by the local press soon after the sale of the Cavern in November 1970.

> *After hearing pop music almost every day for five years as owner of the Cavern, Mr. Alf Geoghegan is now busy writing music himself.*

Alf, who gave up the ownership of the Cavern in November, is doing his best to burst into the song-writing business.

"I'm starting to feel my way about," says Alf. "It's a challenge to succeed at something I have always been interested in."

Alf first started writing songs in 1943 when he was a member of the Ukulele Rhythm Boys on BBC programmes like Workers Playtime *and* Music While You Work.

"I wrote songs to suit our voices because we were desperate for numbers," he says. "I've been writing songs ever since, but only as a hobby until now."

Alf sings or hums the tunes on tapes at his home in Greenbank Road, Mossley Hill – he doesn't write music – and then takes the tapes to Fred Lloyd, organist with the Mal Craig Three.

"I'd like to get somewhere with my work one day, but I won't cry if I don't"

I'm pleased to say that the demise of the Cavern was not the end and, like a Phoenix rising from the ashes, the Cavern we know today is as near to the original as it could possibly be. Each time I visit I'm transported back to the heady days of the Swinging Sixties.

Nigel and I were invited to the Cavern on 16th January 1997 to celebrate its 40th anniversary.

Facing the Cavern on the opposite side of Mathew Street is a wall of bricks inscribed with the names of every group that ever played the

---

THE DIRECTORS OF THE CAVERN
The Most Famous Club in the World
request the pleasure of the company of

Nigel and Debbie Greenberg

on the occasion of
The Cavern's 40th Anniversary Party
at The Cavern, 10 Mathew Street, Liverpool
on Thursday 16th January 1997

R.S.V.P. by 6th January
Cavern City Tours Ltd
The Cavern, 10 Mathew Street
Liverpool, L2 6RE
Tel: 0151 236 9091

12 noon-7.30 p.m.
See over for programme

Cavern. A separate panel of bricks is inscribed with the names of every owner of the Cavern from its opening in 1957 to the present day.

Hats off to Dave Jones and Bill Heckle, the present owners of the Cavern, who have done a wonderful job not only resurrecting the soul of the original Cavern but ensuring that the musical heritage of Mersey Beat survives for future generations, just as my Dad intended.

Panel of bricks listing all Cavern owners

Life After the Cavern

After I left the Club I worked as a beautician for Estee Lauder at Henderson's department store in Liverpool. It was April 1972 and I'd been there about a year when Dad rang me at work, most unusual for him.

"How would you like to run your own business?" he asked.

"I'd love to," I replied.

"Hang on, you don't know what it is yet."

"I don't care what it is, it's got to be better than working for somebody else."

"I'll talk to you when you get home," he said.

I had met my first husband, Greg, at Henderson's and he had since left Liverpool to pursue a career in management at C&A's department store in Birmingham. We were due to be married in June 1972 and Dad put a proposition to us about taking over the running of his taxi garage. He would bring us in as partners so he could step back.

We jumped at the chance, even though neither of us knew the boot of a taxi from its bonnet. Once again I embarked on another adventure and a new learning curve.

Dad was constantly being pestered by taxi drivers wanting to buy parts. He kept a basic supply for the running repairs of his own cabs but he now saw a market niche for supplying the Liverpool taxi trade with spare parts. We had the space to stock them, so off we went for a meeting with British Leyland in Coventry. They agreed to supply us with a full range of taxi spare parts, including body panels.

It wasn't long before we'd built up a chain of account customers that we supplied on twice-daily delivery service.

We supplied Connolly's, Harry Boggs, Taxifix, Standard Radiator Co. a new kid on the block, George Gawith, and many others. At first we couldn't afford a van so I delivered orders in my MG Midget sports car.

When delivering a body panel, I had to lower the top and stack the thing on the small backseat – not a brilliant idea when it rained.

We couldn't afford to offer credit to start with, so it was cash on delivery and for the first few months until we could offer them account facilities.

Delivering parts one time to Billy Lynch's garage, Taxifix, I told the mechanic our policy. He called in Billy Lynch.

"You'll get your money next time, just leave us the parts," said Billy.

"Sorry Billy, no money, no parts. I'm trying to build up an accounts service for the cab industry but we've put all our money into buying stock. I need you to help by paying on delivery for the first few months."

"Wait there," he said, disappearing into the garage.

I thought: that's torn it, I've lost my first account customer, but he returned with cheque in hand.

"Here, I like your style," he said, winking.

It wasn't long before I knew every part and part number of a Hackney cab from boot to bonnet. Eventually we bought a van and employed a delivery driver, store manager and secretary. We were also buying and selling new and used cabs.

It was a whole new world. We owned thirty-one cabs, all of which were hired out to local operators. It was practically a full-time job keeping track of drivers and cab repairs. Whatever was wrong with their cabs – a lost screw or total engine failure – the explanation was invariably the same:

"Me cab fell over."

It took the cabbies a long time to accept that a girl could possibly know what she was talking about regarding the workings of a cab but they eventually realised that I did know my stuff.

We offered trade discounts to all owner drivers, some of whom had several taxis. From my office behind the sales counter one day I overheard a conversation between Greg and a man asking for trade prices. He said he had three cabs. Greg took his details and said he'd let him know.

I rang my mum that evening and asked her what was the name of the man who absconded with Dad's taxi in the 1950s after only one payment and if she could remember where he lived.

"Why do you ask?" She was always inquisitive.

"No reason, I just heard somebody's name mentioned in conversation today, it's not important."

Bingo! The name matched, and so did the address. This was the infamous Mr. Murphy.

Sometimes karma is instant. Sometimes it takes twenty-five years. The strategy here was: "Don't get mad, get even."

I told Greg to add 20% to the trade price and to give him a 10% discount and to put the 10% in an envelope each time Mr. Murphy made a purchase. It took a year or so to accumulate what seemed a fair amount. Then I put it all in an envelope and took it over to my Dad in Wales.

"That's for you, from Mr. Murphy."

"Who's Mr Murphy?" He was bemused.

"Do you remember that guy that ran off with your cab after only one payment in the 1950s?"

"Yes," he said, still confused.

"He's been a customer of ours for over a year now and I figured he owed you, so I've been adding something on to his bill each time he bought parts from us. He's still been getting trade discount and doesn't know he's paid you back, so go and buy that snooker table you want and every time you play you can think of him."

"You little monkey." Dad was laughing, secretly thrilled that Murphy had finally got his comeuppance.

Dad was at last able to retire and enjoy the fruits of his labour, but not before he'd built a huge two storey extension on his house in Wales and he could finally indulge in his passion for the arts. There were very few media he didn't try – oils with brush and palette knife, water colours, pastels, charcoal, acrylics and Indian ink for sketching. I am very happy to enjoy his paintings today. Also an accomplished sculptor, he created a bust of my head which I treasure.

All his life he had wanted a horse and considered buying one and keeping it in the barn that was attached to two cottages that he owned across the lane from his home in Wales. He said he would look after it and I could ride it when I visited them.

I was working full time in the taxi garage when mum and dad retired to Wales, as usual I had taken over the business for him and although it was a very tempting offer it wouldn't have been fair to the horse, as I wouldn't have been able to see it regularly.

I am mad about animals and even though I had never had a great deal of experience with horses it didn't stop me loving them. Some years earlier, Greg and I had joined a party of friends at The Grand National. We were in the main stand close to the winning post and were spared some of the awful sights of injured horses that had fallen during the race.

Dad always used to give a tip for the winner of the Grand National when he was in the butcher's in North Hill Street and would write his prediction in whitewash on the shop window for his customers.

I can only remember one instance when he got it wrong. He had had a dream the night before the race and awoke with the message, 'One in the middle and one at each end.' He scoured the newspapers over and over again but just couldn't make the connection. When 'Ayala' won, it was so obvious that my Dad said, "How could I have possibly missed that?" he couldn't believe it and to add insult to injury, one of our butcher boys called Terry Duffy said he had backed it to win after what my Dad had said.

Dad asked him why he hadn't told him and is reply was, "I thought you would have spotted it."

Dad was hurt that Terry hadn't shared his thoughts with him; after all he had unwittingly given him the tip. To this day we still say "one in the middle and one at each end" whenever we hear Ayala's name mentioned. These days, I can't bear to watch the Grand National, it upsets me too much when the horses are hurt.

In December 1979 I divorced my husband but I stayed on in the business until my Dad and I sold our shares to my ex in the summer of 1980.

Billy Lynch, my first account customer was the only one who came to see me at our garage. He'd heard that my husband and I were parting ways and asked if there was anything at all he could do to help."

"Money, time, advice, just ask," he offered.

That meant such a lot to me, even though I didn't need to call on him for anything. He had taken the trouble and the time to come up to Prescot where our garage was, some nine miles from his garage in Liverpool to offer me his help. What a great guy, thank you Billy.

I had been invited to a dinner party at the home of some friends one Saturday evening in April 1981. They asked me to bring someone if I wanted to. I had been anti-men since my divorce so I told them there was nobody I wanted to bring and so my friend, Eunice, who was also my hairdresser asked if they could invite someone for me.

"Edward's got a friend; he's Jewish, divorced, two kids," she hinted.

"Woah, Don't be setting me up with anybody," I said

"Look, if you don't like him, at the end of the evening you can go your separate ways.

Immediately I had the vision of Jewish man wearing a large black hat with payas (long side curls of hair) hanging down his face. My vision couldn't have been further from the truth. I was pleasantly surprised.

It transpired that the blind date was with Nigel Greenberg, who not only knew my Mum and Dad but had owned the recording studio at the Cavern before we owned the Club. We had never actually met, though we had both attended several of the same functions in the past.

He was also the guy that had fixed the electrics when we had the blackout on the opening day of the Cavern. We were like ships that passed in the night.

Needless to say, by 2 a.m. Nigel and I were still talking and our hosts were falling asleep.

"Here's the keys, lock up when you've finished talking and push the keys through the letterbox, we're going to bed," Edward said. "I've got a golf tournament in the morning."

Dad was delighted to meet Nigel again but unfortunately they didn't have much time together before my Dad died suddenly in July 1981. They got on so well together and I know they could have had some good times ahead but it wasn't to be.

It was the 5th July 1981, the night of the Toxteth riots. Nigel and I had been to see a film at the Odeon Cinema in London Road and on the way home we drove through town towards Upper Parliament Street.

As we approached the Rialto we couldn't believe our eyes. There were fires burning everywhere, the Rialto was ablaze, riot police were running around carrying protective shields and trying to abate the riot but there were too few of them and the situation was out of control. Because we had already driven halfway across the road before realising the severity of the mayhem around us, Nigel put his foot down and dodged the embers and the police. We had been lucky to come through it unscathed.

When we arrived home at my house, the telephone was ringing. It was a neighbour of my parents who said that my Dad had been rushed into Glan Clwyd Hospital in Wales. My Mum and Dad had been living in Wales for the past nine years in a cottage they had bought several years before and had used as a holiday home.

I was frantic. I couldn't take the news in. I had only been speaking to my Dad that afternoon before Nigel and I had gone to the cinema. We spoke to each other every day.

My Dad's Daf car was still parked outside my house and because it had a full tank of petrol and was automatic we took it. Nigel drove like a bat out of hell and we made it to the hospital in just over an hour. Neither of us remember the journey it was a complete blur.

I was able to see Dad briefly before the nurses ushered us out of the room. He died later that night.

He was my rock, my friend, my mentor. He was the kindest, sweetest soul with a big heart but above all he was my Dad and I love and miss him very much. His sister Lyn says he was as strong as an ox, a tough little guy with a big brain.

During the first week in May 1981, Nigel was travelling back from London to Liverpool by train after attending IFSEC, a security trade exhibition at Earls Court. A little while after he had settled into his seat in the dining carriage, he heard someone shouting to him and waving from further down the carriage.

"Alright, Nige?"

It was Mike McCartney. On his way towards Nigel he stopped to talk to someone for a few minutes and then finally joined up with him.

"Sorry about that, I had to stop and talk to to Harold (Harold Wilson), I couldn't walk past and not say hello." Mike joined Nigel at his table.

"I'm glad I've seen you, you don't know anyone who would do a wedding video, do you? Rowena and I are getting married at the end of May and our kid (Paul McCartney) is coming up for the wedding, so it would have to be discreet."

"I'll film it for you, I've got a small video production company, just give me a ring with the details."

"That's brilliant, thanks Nige." They shook hands and Mike returned to his seat.

The following day, Mike rang Nigel with the details for the wedding. The wedding was to take place on 31st May 1981 at St Barnabas's church in Penny Lane in Liverpool. Nigel asked Mike if he could bring his girlfriend Debbie along who would be 'key grip' on the day, for the production of the video and gave his assurance that she would be equally as discreet.

"Of course you can, not a problem, see you on the day." Mike said.

Nigel visited St Barnabas's church to introduce himself to the vicar and to explain what would be happening. He was happy to accept the videoing outside the church but was adamant that no filming whatsoever was to take place inside the church.

The morning of the wedding arrived, it was a beautiful day, the sun was shining, a perfect day for filming. Nigel and I arrived outside the church at least an hour before the service began and already people had started to gather around the main entrance at the front of the church in Penny Lane.

Mike had told Nigel that the wedding party would be leaving the church by the rear door In Elm Hall Drive. We sat in the car for as long as possible before setting up the camera outside the rear door of the church because we knew that if someone saw a film crew they would realise what was happening.

We had barely had the chance to set up the equipment when a torrent of excited onlookers flooded around the corner of the church from Penny Lane to where we were positioned in Elm Hall Drive outside the rear entrance to the church. We could hear them coming long before they came into view. It wasn't long before the road was bursting at the seams.

Cameras at the ready, everybody was anxious to get a bird's eye view of the bride and groom and of course their idol Paul and his wife Linda.

We had to make sure that we were right at the front to capture every moment of this memorable occasion.

It seemed to take forever for the doors of the church to open. Finally they were slowly prised apart and out stepped some of the guests followed as if in slow motion by more guests, then the bridesmaids, more guests and at last the bride and groom. Mike and Rowena looked so happy, she looked absolutely radiant in a beautiful cream satin and lace gown scattered with tiny pearls that glistened in the midday sun. It had a fitted bodice to the

Paul and Linda at Mike and Rowena's wedding with Aunty Gin

waist with long sleeves and a lace panel at the neck-line which gave way to a full and billowing floor-length dream of a dress. Her short hair was adorned with a tasteful headdress and veil and she wore delicate drop ear rings. She carried a bouquet of yellow and cream roses.

Mike looked very dapper in a light grey suit. The bridesmaids were dressed in two-tiered, full-skirted knee-length dresses in lemon satin and carried smaller bouquets of yellow and cream roses.

Finally, after hanging back so as not to steal the show, Paul and Linda stepped out of the shadows and into the limelight. The crowd went wild, girls were screaming, cameras were clicking, Nigel and I were being pushed around desperately trying to keep our balance and at the same time concentrating on keeping the film rolling.

Paul was wearing a navy blue jacket and trousers a cream shirt, loosely arranged at the neck by a green tie dotted with splashes of coloured stripes and triangles in black, white, yellow and red. He wore white trainers on his feet. Linda wore a simply tailored V-necked knee-length dress in white, belted at the waist and decorated with tiny sprigs of red roses and wore red sandals. She wore a single strand of pearls at her neck and wore no make-up. They both looked extremely laid back.

The crowd was increasing in numbers and noise by the minute, shouts of, "Paul, over here, Paul look this way, give us a wave, love yer, Paul."

The wedding party gave the crowd a good amount of time for photo shots before the wedding car inched its way through the crowds towards the bottom of the church steps. Mike had used his own car to collect them from the church, a racing green Bristol.

Rowena and Mike slowly and carefully made their way down the church steps to the waiting car. Paul's chauffeur-driven Volvo estate car inched in behind to take Paul and Linda, who by this time were adept at making exits through crowds and cleverly manoeuvred their way through the crowd and into their waiting car.

A further car arrived to take the bridesmaids on to the reception.

Once all the guests had left the church Nigel and I stopped filming and made our way by car to the reception.

Paul and Linda with Nigel and Debbie

The reception was held in a marquee in the garden of Mike's home on the Wirral. It was a very relaxed atmosphere. After half an hour or so of arriving Mike and Rowena cut their wedding cake and Paul and Mike launched into an impromptu rendering of 'Bye Bye Love,' by the Everly Brothers, which triggered a playful look of disapproval from Rowena and a burst of laughter from the guests.

A buffet was laid on for guests to help themselves to food and the champagne was flowing.

As it was such a beautiful day many people gathered around in the garden. Paul was catching up with his cousin, Ted Robbins, telling jokes, enjoying a drink too many and getting a telling-off from a then-twelve-year-old Stella. Linda was pushing James, who was two years old, on the garden swing, it was such a relaxed happy atmosphere and all the time Nigel and I continued to video the reception for Mike and Rowena. Several hours later before guests started to take their leave, Paul sat at the piano which had been carried into the marquee and started to play and sing 'Ebony and Ivory.' It was magical, everybody joined in with him. It was such an historic moment.

Soon after that Paul and Linda left the reception, and still filming, we followed them outside the house while they loaded up their dark blue estate car with all their bags and their children, and after waving goodbye to everyone they sped off down the road and out of sight.

We went back into the reception to thank Mike and Rowena for their hospitality and Nigel told Mike to phone him when they got back from their honeymoon and arrange a day to collect the tape from him.

We consider ourselves to be very privileged to have been asked to film Mike and Rowena's wedding and completely respect their privacy.

We left the reception on a high and couldn't wait to get back home and view the video. It was a wonderful record of an amazing day.

In May 2006, Nigel and I were at a Charity function in St George's Hall in Liverpool enjoying a welcome drink, and who walks in but Mike McCartney. He came straight over to us.

"Aright Nige, I can't believe you're here tonight. I've just been talking to our kid (Paul) this afternoon about you. It's our Silver Wedding in a few weeks and he's putting on a party for us at The Savoy in London and none of us can find the tape you did of our wedding, I don't suppose you've still got the master have you?"

"I certainly have, it's under lock and key, I'll make you a copy." Nigel offered.

"Thanks that's brilliant, you know, a lot of the people on that tape are no longer with us, it would be great to see them all again." Mike was thrilled.

"Isn't it a coincidence that Deb and I were here tonight," Nigel said

Mike's reply was, "There's no such thing as coincidence."

A few weeks later, Mike and Rowena called to our house on their way down to London to pick up the tape and brought us a bottle of bubbly to say thanks.

To this day we have never shown the tape of their wedding to a soul and would never do so without their permission.

Our Beatles connection continued to bear fruit for others. In May 1983 Nigel and I were contacted by our friend Stephen Maycock, who worked at Sotheby's auction house. He asked if Mark Lewisohn, an author and Beatles specialist, could consult with us to verify some facts for a book he was writing about the Beatles' live performances.

When he called in to see us, we showed him the posters and handbills we had kept from earlier Beatles performances before they were famous. One particular poster that interested him was too large to be photographed locally so, as Mark was returning to London the next morning, I offered to let him take it to be processed for inclusion in his book, *The Beatles Live!* He duly returned the poster by return post.

Since then Mark has written many books about the Beatles and is now considered one of the world's leading specialists on the subject.

I had retired when I met Nigel, or so I thought. Who was I kidding? It wasn't long before I was involved in the running of Nigel's business, Solo Security. We were married in June 1984 and thirty-five years on from our first meeting we're still buzzing with conversation. We thrive on work and challenge and change. Dad always used to say to me, "Never be afraid of change, change is progress."

How right he was, he gave me the best advice I have ever had in my life. "It's not what life deals you, it's how you deal with it that matters, and always remember that the quickest way to solve a problem is to go straight through the middle of it."

My Mum told me that he had said to her "If I'd had three sons they mightn't have turned out as good as Deb." I had an excellent teacher in him and I am eternally grateful.

I can remember thanking him for all the good advice he had given me over the years, his reply was," You didn't have to take it."

Nigel and I are still in business, Solo Security is now in its forty-fifth year and continues to go from strength to strength.

Lightning Source UK Ltd.
Milton Keynes UK
UKHW020835280719
346922UK00005B/208/P